What people are saying about

Decoding Jung's Metaphysics

What I appreciate most about Bernardo Kastrup's approach is his recognition that the tools of philosophy can help us approach the depth, the gift of analytic psychology and appreciate its contributions. ... Kastrup's decoding of Jung's profound insights adds another layer to our understanding. Rather than see, post-Kant, metaphysics as wistful speculation, one sees that the meta-physis engagement has moved within, where it always was.
James Hollis, Ph.D., Jungian analyst and best-selling author

Bernardo Kastrup's rigorous analysis and penetrating insights are paving the way for an important, and truly massive, shift in our understanding of the relationship between consciousness and what we think of as the physical world. His approach is both subtle and wise. His persistent scholarship in this area makes evident points of metaphysical clarification that even Jung, himself, was hesitant to explicate.
Jeffrey Mishlove, Ph.D., psychologist and host of Thinking Allowed

T0167504

Decoding Jung's Metaphysics

The archetypal semantics of
an experiential universe

Decoding Jung's Metaphysics

The archetypal semantics of
an experiential universe

Bernardo Kastrup

Foreword by Jeffrey Mishlove
Afterword by James Hollis

IFF
BOOKS

Winchester, UK
Washington, USA

JOHN HUNT PUBLISHING

First published by iff Books, 2021
iff Books is an imprint of John Hunt Publishing Ltd., No. 3 East Street, Alresford,
Hampshire SO24 9EE, UK
office@jhpbooks.com
www.johnhuntpublishing.com
www.iff-books.com

For distributor details and how to order please visit the 'Ordering' section on our website.

ISBN: 978 1 78904 565 9
978 1 78904 566 6 (ebook)
Library of Congress Control Number: 2019956137

Printed and bound by CPI Group (UK) Ltd, Croydon, CR0 4YY

Contents

Other books by Bernardo Kastrup

Rationalist Spirituality: An exploration of the meaning of life and existence informed by logic and science

Dreamed up Reality: Diving into mind to uncover the astonishing hidden tale of nature

Meaning in Absurdity: What bizarre phenomena can tell us about the nature of reality

Why Materialism Is Baloney: How true skeptics know there is no death and fathom answers to life, the universe, and everything

Brief Peeks Beyond: Critical essays on metaphysics, neuroscience, free will, skepticism and culture

More Than Allegory: On religious myth, truth and belief

The Idea of the World: A multi-disciplinary argument for the mental nature of reality

Decoding Schopenhauer's Metaphysics: The key to understanding how it solves the hard problem of consciousness and the paradoxes of quantum mechanics

List of acronyms

Jung's works are referred to as follows:

A: Jung, C. G. (1979). *Aion, 2ⁿᵈ Ed.* Princeton, NJ: Princeton University Press.

AA: Jung, C. G., Pauli, W. (authors) and Meier, C. A. (editor) (2001). *Atom and Archetype: The Pauli/Jung Letters 1932-1958.* London, UK: Routledge.

ACU: Jung, C. G. (1991). *The Archetypes and the Collective Unconscious.* London, UK: Routledge.

AJ: Jung, C. G. (2002). *Answer to Job.* London, UK: Routledge.

D: Jung, C. G. (2001). *Dreams.* London, UK: Routledge.

FS: Jung, C. G. (1978). *Flying Saucers: A Modern Myth of Things Seen in the Skies.* Princeton, NJ: Princeton University Press.

JWL: Jung, C. G., White, V. (authors), Lammers, A. C. and Cunningham, A. (editors) (2007). *The Jung-White Letters.* London, UK: Routledge.

L: Jung, C. G. (author), Adler, G. and Jaffé, A. (editors) (1975). *C. G. Jung Letters.* Princeton, NJ: Princeton University Press.

MDR: Jung, C. G. (author) and Jaffé, A. (editor) (1995). *Memories, Dreams, Reflections.* London, UK: Fontana Press.

MMSS: Jung, C. G. (2001). *Modern Man in Search of a Soul.* London, UK: Routledge.

ONP: Jung, C. G. (2001). *On the Nature of the Psyche.* London, UK: Routledge.

PA: Jung, C. G. (1980). *Psychology and Alchemy, 2ⁿᵈ Edition.* London, UK: Routledge.

PR: Jung, C. G. (1977). *Psychology and Religion.* New Haven, CT: Yale University Press.

RB: Jung, C. G. (author) and Shamdasani, S. (editor) (2009).

The Red Book: Liber Novus. London, UK: W. W. Norton & Company.

S: Jung, C. G. (1985). *Synchronicity: An Acausal Connecting Principle*. London, UK: Routledge.

US: Jung, C. G. (2002). *The Undiscovered Self*. London, UK: Routledge.

Conforming to the divine will I live for mankind, not only for myself, and whoever understands this message contained in and conveyed by my writing will also live for me.

Carl Gustav Jung

Foreword by Jeffrey Mishlove

I have had the privilege of spending satisfying hours with Bernardo Kastrup exploring both his penetrating metaphysical philosophy as well as his deep dives into realms of active imagination and mythos. This was accomplished at a distance of thousands of miles, recorded on video, for the *New Thinking Allowed* YouTube channel. So, although we have never met face-to-face, I believe I am somewhat justified in feeling that I have been inside of Bernardo's mind. I suspect that many viewers, and readers, worldwide, also share this feeling.

Bernardo brings his rigorous background as a computer scientist to his analysis of consciousness and reality. He achieved a measure of renown by publishing articles advocating idealist metaphysics on the *Scientific American* website. Then, after having published seven books for the educated public explicating the fine details of his thinking, he determined to test his ideas in the mill of academia by earning a second doctoral degree—this time in philosophy. I believe that Bernardo's vital drive, his entelechy or purpose, is to engage with the ultimate questions in philosophy and psychology using the finely-honed tools of logic. In so doing, he is also well aware of the limits of such logic—especially when turning inward to examine his own psychic depths. This book, *Decoding Jung's Metaphysics*, is in part, I believe, Bernardo's admirable effort to reconcile logic with that which is beyond all logic.

As a parapsychologist, my own interest in metaphysics and the philosophy of mind has been stimulated by empirical data gathered by skilled researchers starting in 1882 when the Society for Psychical Research was first formed in England. Many distinguished scientists and philosophers have been associated with this research endeavor—including such well-known figures as William James, Sir Oliver Lodge, Sir William Crookes, Nobel

1

laureate Charles Richet, and philosopher Henri Bergson. The discipline of psychical research initially developed using the methodologies of field research and case studies. A significant focus of these studies was the claim of human survival of bodily death, brought to the forefront of public attention because of a massive global interest in the phenomena associated with nineteenth century spiritualism.

In the twentieth century, as psychical researchers began paying more attention to the advances in experimental science and statistics, both the nomenclature and the thinking began to change. Joseph Banks Rhine, working in the psychology department at Duke University in the 1930s, popularized the term 'extra sensory perception' — more commonly known as ESP. Rhine, and his colleagues, also designated the term *psi* as a generic word covering all of the various manifestations (i.e., telepathy, clairvoyance, precognition, and psychokinesis) studied by the discipline for which they chose the label 'parapsychology.'

The important questions concerning human post-mortem survival did not go away. However, J. B. Rhine, himself, was disillusioned with séances and the spiritualist mentality. Furthermore, it seemed as if all of the best evidence in support of the survival hypothesis could be explained more parsimoniously as living agent psi.

The *Journal of Parapsychology* was founded in 1937 and has been published continuously since then. In 1957, the Parapsychological Association was founded and, in 1969, that association formally became an affiliate of the American Association for the Advancement of Science — by virtue of a vote by the governing council of the AAAS.

Carl Jung, himself, had an abiding interest in parapsychological phenomena. Jung's doctoral dissertation, published in 1903, was titled *"On the Psychology and Pathology of So-Called Occult Phenomena."* He corresponded with J. B. Rhine and, in his classic essay on synchronicity, he repeatedly referred to Rhine's parapsychology experiments and how important they were. In fact, in a private communication to Rhine, on September 3, 1951, Jung confessed that his essay on synchronicity (presented to the Eranos Foundation that year) was "largely based on your ESP experiment."

For his part, Rhine was hesitant to embrace an acausal model of psi. Research, such as the 'sheep-goat effect' in parapsychology, suggested that psi operated in a manner consistent with known psychological variables, in particular it was influenced by belief systems. Nevertheless, some parapsychologists had more than a passing interest in Jung's hypothesis. In spite of the fact that hundreds of well-conducted empirical experiments had demonstrated the existence of psi, the Rhinean model of extra sensory perception encountered serious difficulties. No biological organ appeared to be associated with extra sensory perception. Nor has anyone discovered a channel of information transmission that could account for the many highly accurate and detailed accounts produced in clairvoyant research. Some parapsychologists, such as John Palmer in his 1979 presidential address to the Parapsychological Association, have seriously proposed that the Jungian model of synchronicity may be a better fit for the data than the Rhinean notion of extra sensory perception.

J. B. Rhine, himself, understood this dilemma. In 1965, when he left his position at Duke University, Rhine founded a new organization in Durham, North Carolina, that he called the Foundation for Research on the Nature of Man. (That organization is currently known as the Rhine Research Center.) I understand that he chose this name because he realized that the data he and his colleagues had been collecting for decades could not be adequately explained from within the prevalent materialistic paradigm. The phrase, "Research on the Nature of Man," was meant to imply that empirical studies of parapsychology pointed to something about human nature that was essentially different than the common scientific supposition.

Of course, it is no secret that—in spite of its many contributions to human understanding—parapsychology remains a fringe science. I know this in my bones, having earned a unique, interdisciplinary doctoral diploma (from the University of California, Berkeley, 1980) that actually states my field of study as 'parapsychology.' To my knowledge, no other accredited university in the world has ever issued such a diploma either before or since. I do not wish to make too much of my lonely distinction. After all, there are about 400 members of the Parapsychological Association today. Many of them have earned doctoral degrees in 'psychology' or 'philosophy' for dissertations on parapsychological topics. Yet almost all of these individuals have shared personal stories regarding prejudicial treatment they have received because of their interest in the paranormal. For example, one such individual—a Nobel laureate physicist— was disinvited from a professional conference in physics due to this interest.

Carl Jung, however, did not share such a prejudice. In an invited address to the Society for Psychical Research in 1919, he uttered the following memorable words: "I shall not commit the fashionable stupidity of regarding everything that I cannot explain as a fraud." Unfortunately, from my perspective, many of those who call themselves Jungians do not share Jung's courageous attitude. I have spoken to prominent Jungians who maintain that synchronicity is quite distinct from parapsychological phenomena.

The situation is far worse, however, in academia. Topics such as metaphysical idealism and panpsychism are, commendably, gaining ground within professional philosophy. The study of consciousness itself is becoming ever more respectable within departments of psychology. Nevertheless, there is still an unmistakable tendency for scholars in these areas to act as if 140 years of empirical investigations in psychical research and parapsychology did not even exist!

It is worth mentioning, however, that there is now a notable exception to this blackout of knowledge. In August of 2018, the flagship journal of the American Psychological Association, *The American Psychologist*, published an article by Etzel Cardeña, a professor of psychology at Lund University, Sweden, titled "The Experimental Evidence for Parapsychological Phenomena: A Review." This article summarized several meta-analyses covering over 1,400 parapsychological experiments and concluded that, at its best, psi research exhibits methodological excellence and promising results.

The Cardeña article accentuates what I have believed throughout my professional career: that the time is long overdue for the empirical data of parapsychology and its implications to be integrated into the mainstream canon of academic and philosophical knowledge. Although Bernardo Kastrup does not address this issue directly in this book, his rigorous analysis and penetrating insights are paving the way for an important, and truly massive, shift in our understanding of the relationship between consciousness and what we think of as the physical world. His approach is both subtle and wise. His persistent scholarship in this area makes evident points of metaphysical clarification that even Jung, himself, was hesitant to explicate.

Jeffrey Mishlove, Ph.D.
Albuquerque, New Mexico.

Chapter 1

Prelude

Call it not vain — that lofty thought
Which peoples heaven with visioned lore,
So that each star of light is fraught
With some fair chronicle of yore: —
Call it not vain, though earthly vision
May not peruse that page Elysian,
But strive to read it in vain;
Mind will the links of form supply,
Of forms that never more may die, —
To mind they are all plain.

Leopold J. Bernays, from the poem *The Constellations*, published in the appendix of his translation of Johann Wolfgang von Goethe's *Faust* (1839)

Born on the margins of Lake Constance, in Kesswil, Switzerland, in the summer of 1875, Carl Gustav Jung was one of the most important figures of early modern psychology. Together with Sigmund Freud, he pioneered the systematic exploration of the depths of the human psyche beyond the threshold of direct introspection, a mysterious realm he and Freud called 'the unconscious.' Both men discerned tremendous significance in aspects of our inner lives that had hitherto been neglected by science, particularly dreams.

However, unlike Freud — who thought of the unconscious as merely a passive repository of forgotten or repressed contents of consciousness — for Jung the unconscious was an *active, creative matrix* with a psychic life, will and language of its own, often at odds with our conscious dispositions. It is this aspect of his thinking that led Jung down avenues of empirical investigation and speculation rich with metaphysical significance. This little book is about those extraordinary speculations and their philosophical implications.

As we shall soon find out, for Jung life and world are something very different from what our present mainstream metaphysics—materialism—posits. The conclusions of his lifelong studies point to the continuation of psychic life beyond bodily death, a much more intimate and direct relationship between matter and psyche than most would dare imagine today, and a living universe pregnant with symbolic meaning. For him life is, quite literally, a kind of dream, and interpretable as such.

Jung was many things: psychiatrist, psychologist, historian, classicist, mythologist, painter, sculptor and even—as some would argue with good reasons—a mystic (cf. e.g. Kingsley 2018). But he expressly avoided identifying himself as a philosopher, lest such a label detract from the image of empirical scientist that he wanted to project. Nonetheless, much of what Jung had to say about the psyche has unavoidable and rather remarkable philosophical implications, not only concerning the mind-body problem, but also the very nature of reality itself. Moreover, when he was being less guarded—which was often—Jung made overt philosophical statements. For these reasons, as I hope to make clear in this book, Jung ultimately proved to be a philosopher, even a very good one.

In the pages that follow, I shall first attempt to tease out the most important metaphysical *implications* of Jung's ideas on the nature and behavior of the psyche. Second, I shall try to relate Jung's many overt metaphysical contentions to those implications. Third, based on the previous two points, I shall try to reconstruct what I believe to have been Jung's implicit metaphysical system, demonstrating its internal consistency, as well as its epistemic and empirical adequacy. I shall argue that Jung was a metaphysical idealist in the tradition of German

Idealism, his system being particularly consistent with that of Arthur Schopenhauer and my own.

The consistency between Jung's metaphysics and my own is no coincidence. Unlike Schopenhauer—whose work I've discovered only after having developed my system in seven different books—Jung has been a very early influencer of my thought. I first came across his work still in my early teens, during a family holiday in the mountains. Exploring on my own the village where we were staying, I chanced upon a small bookshop. There, displayed very prominently, was an intriguing book titled *I Ching*, edited and translated by Richard Wilhelm, with a foreword by one Carl Gustav Jung. Jung's introduction to the book revealed the internal logic and root of plausibility of what I would otherwise have regarded as just a silly oracle. He had opened some kind of door in my mind. Little did I know, then, how far that door would eventually take me.

Jung's hand in my work can probably be discerned in many more passages than I myself am aware of, for I have internalized his thought so deeply over the years that I don't doubt I sometimes conflate his ideas with mine. Moreover, Jung's image has been a perennial presence in both my intellectual and emotional inner lives. In moments of stress, anxiety or hopelessness, I often visualize myself in conversation with him—he would have called it 'active imagination'—so as to envision what he would have had to say about my situation. This level of intimacy hopefully helps me represent Jung's thought accurately and fairly in this volume. The reader should have no doubt that doing so is of utmost importance to me.

Naturally, it is also conceivable that the same intimacy could hamper my objectivity, leading me—surreptitiously and unintentionally—to pass an idiosyncratic amalgamation of his views *and mine* for his metaphysics. To guard against this risk, I've re-read—for the third or fourth time in my life—all of Jung's relevant works in preparation for writing this volume. I have also reproduced relevant excerpts of Jung's writings to substantiate my case, only making assertions I could trace back to *multiple* passages in their corresponding context. This, I hope, ensures the objectivity and accuracy of my interpretations.

Jung has written over twenty thick volumes of material over his long and productive life. Much of it is limited to clinical psychology or mythology and has little metaphysical significance. The material that *does* have metaphysical relevance, however, is still quite extensive.

So whenever Jung's views changed—substantially or simply in terms of nuances—over the years, I have prioritized his later writing. In addition, Jung's metaphysical views seem to have congealed only towards the end of his professional life, which renders his earlier writings less relevant. For these two reasons, my argument is based mostly on works he wrote from the 1940s onwards, with two exceptions: the edited transcripts of his *Terry Lectures*, held at Yale University in 1937-1938 (PR), and a collection of essays published in 1933 (MMSS). Both provide tantalizing early insights into Jung's growing confidence regarding his metaphysical views.

It is important to notice that, regardless of the period in which it was written, Jung's discourse on metaphysics and related topics comes nowhere near the level of conceptual clarity, consistency and precision that today's analytic philosophers demand. Jung was an extremely intuitive thinker who favored analogies, similes and metaphors over direct and unambiguous exposition, appearing to frequently contradict himself. This happened because he didn't use linear argument structures, but instead *circumambulated*—a handy Jungian term meaning 'to walk round about'—the topic in question in an effort to convey the full gamut of his intuitions about it. Indeed, he didn't arrive at his views purely through steps of reasoning to begin with, but largely through visionary experience (cf. MDR: 217 & 225, RB). It is thus only natural that he should express these views in an intuitive, analogical manner.

In this context, Jung's many seeming contradictions reflect attempts to explore a theme from several different perspectives and reference points. For instance, if he claims that the psyche is material, just to turn around and say that it is spiritual, he means that *there is a sense* in which the psyche is analogous to what we call 'matter' and *another sense* in which it is analogous to what we call 'spirit,' each sense anchored in its own implicit reference point. It is these radical and sudden flips of perspective—confusing and aggravating for an analytic disposition as they are—that help Jung delineate and express his views in a way that appeals to more than just reason.

Before closing this brief introduction, a few notes on terminology are required. Throughout this book—unless otherwise stated—I try to stick to the same terms and denotations that Jung himself used, even though his terminology is now largely outdated. I've done so to maintain consistency with his corpus. For instance, Jung defines 'consciousness' as something considerably more specific than what philosophers today refer to as 'phenomenal consciousness' or simply 'consciousness' (this, in fact, has been the source of endless misunderstandings of Jung's work). So, unless I explicitly write 'phenomenal consciousness,' I use the terms 'consciousness' and 'conscious' according to Jung's own restrictive definition.

Some of the other terms I use have both colloquial and technical philosophical meanings, which unfortunately differ. I try to consistently use those terms in their *technical* sense. By the term 'metaphysics,' for instance, I don't mean supernatural entities or paranormal phenomena, but the *essence of being* of things, creatures and phenomena. As such, a metaphysics of nature entails a certain view about what nature *is* in and of itself, as opposed to how it *behaves* (which is the subject of science) or how it *appears* to observation (which is a subject of cognitive psychology and phenomenology).

But fear not: knowing as I do that much of the readership of this volume will be composed of psychologists, therapists and people generally interested in metaphysics—as opposed to professional philosophers alone—I've striven to keep the jargon to a bare minimum. I also either explicitly define technical terms on first usage or use them in a way that makes their intended meaning clear and unambiguous from the context.

This is only one of many stylistic choices I've made to ensure that this little volume is not only readable, but also clear, compelling and enjoyable to a general readership. I hope you find inspiration in it to, someday, delve more deeply into Jung's extraordinary legacy.

Chapter 2

Psyche

There are three heavens ... These follow in sequence and are interdependent ... The deeper levels of the human mind and disposition are in a similar pattern as well. We have a central, intermediate, and outmost nature. This is because when humanity was created the whole divine design was gathered into it, to the point that as to structure, the human being is the divine design and is therefore a heaven in miniature. For the same reason we are in touch with heaven as to our inner natures ... The outside and the inside in the heavens (or in each particular heaven) are like our own volitional side and its cognitive aspect. ... The volitional is like a flame and the cognitive like the light that it sheds. ... We may therefore conclude that the state of our inner natures is what constitutes heaven and that heaven is within each of us, not outside us.

Emanuel Swedenborg, in *Heaven and Hell* (1758)

The foundational concept underlying all of Jung's work—and all of psychology, for that matter—is that of *psyche*. The term is derived from the Greek ψῡχή—soul—and refers to the human *mind* in the most general and comprehensive sense. Indeed, whereas the word 'mind' is often used—even by Jung himself—in the restrictive sense of intellect or rational thought, 'psyche' has a broader denotation, encompassing not only thought but also intuition, imagination, feeling, emotion, etc.

The precise meaning Jung attributes to the term 'psyche' is of utmost importance for interpreting his metaphysics. The reason is that, for Jung and all depth psychologists, the psyche encompasses not only *conscious* processes, but also *unconscious* ones. The psychic status of the latter must then be explicated and justified, for whereas nobody questions the psychic nature of conscious processes, it is not immediately clear what characterizes an *un*conscious process as psychic. One could argue, for instance, that unconscious processes are merely *physiological* and, as such, of the same material—as opposed to psychic—nature as liver and kidney function.

Jung starts his discussion about the nature of the psyche by first acknowledging that some processes on the boundary between the merely organic and the properly psychic—such as instincts—correlate with physiology. This gives him a lever to begin defining what it means for a process to be psychic:

the psychic is an emancipation of function from its instinctual form ... The psychic condition or quality begins where the function loses its outer and inner determinism and ... begins to show itself accessible to a will motivated from other sources. (ONP: 108)

Psychic processes, therefore, are those amenable—at least to some extent—to *deliberate volition*, as opposed to being entirely determined by instinctual urges grounded in physiology. For instance, whereas a lower animal might compulsively eat all it can because of its physiology-mediated instinctual urge to do so, humans can deliberately choose to eat less than they actually feel like because of some longer-term motivation, such as reducing weight. This deliberate choice—made not only independently from, but even in direct opposition to, instincts—reflects a proper psychic process.

Jung then extends this notion towards the polar opposite of instinct:

with increasing freedom from sheer instinct the [psyche] will ultimately reach a point at which the intrinsic energy of the function ceases altogether to be oriented by instinct in the original sense, and attains a so-called "spiritual" form. (ONP: 109)

This "spiritual form" is

a functional complex which originally, on the primitive level, was felt as an invisible, breath-like "presence." ... spirit makes [man] creative, always spurring him on, ... *takes possession of him,* ... *binds his freedom* (ACU: 210-213, emphasis added)

People who sublimate their instinctual urges in a life of self-abnegation, oriented towards altruistic purposes, embody such spiritual form. When this happens, Jung argues that deliberate volition relinquishes control to impersonal forces that transcend egotistic interests. This is why spirit (the drive to serve something bigger than oneself) is the opposite of instinct (the drive to act towards of one's own survival).

Qualitatively, what characterizes the dynamisms of spirit is that, contrary to instinct, they

often contain a *superior analysis or insight or knowledge* which consciousness has not been able to produce. We have a suitable word for such occurrences — intuition. (PR: 49, emphasis added)

Because "primitive mentality finds it quite natural to personify the invisible presence" (ACU: 210) of spirit, Jung sometimes alludes to these spiritual dispositions as *daemons* — autonomous complexes or agencies with a resolve of their own, which we do not identify with — capable of subjugating psychic life to their own agenda and superior insight (cf. e.g. MDR: 380). He highlights the autonomous nature of these complexes in passages such as this:

It is just as if the complex were an *autonomous being* capable of interfering with the intentions of the ego [i.e. the part of the psyche we identify with and deliberately control]. Complexes indeed behave like secondary or partial personalities *in possession of a mental life of their own*. (PR: 14, emphasis added)

When these autonomous complexes "grow out of the unconscious mind and invade consciousness with their weird and unassailable convictions and impulses" (PR: 14), one becomes 'possessed by a daemon,' so to speak,[1] turning into "a helpless victim" (PR: 14). The altruistic lives of saints, for instance, exemplify the subjugation of our personal volition to the impersonal, superior, spiritual agenda of daemons.

The picture we are then left with is of a psyche sandwiched between instinct on the lower end and spirit on the higher. On the lower end, deliberate personal volition cedes control to the automatism of compulsive drives, whereas on the higher end it is subjugated to the impersonal agenda of daemons. This equates the psyche proper with processes under the control of deliberate personal volition (cf. ONP: 110).

The problem is that defining the psyche in this manner doesn't solve the issue it was meant to address to begin with: insofar as we can't imagine an *unconscious* but still *deliberate* choice, we also cannot conceive of a psychic process that lacks consciousness. So the psyche remains identical with consciousness — as Jung explicitly acknowledges (cf. ONP: 111) — and the psychic status of unconscious processes remains unaccounted for.

To solve this impasse, Jung resorts — at least when he is paying attention and striving for some level of conceptual consistency — to the qualifier 'proper': "What I would call the psyche *proper* extends to all functions which can be brought under the influence of a will" (ONP: 110, emphasis added). This way, insofar as our will influences e.g. our thoughts and imagination, these thoughts and imagination fall within the psychic sphere *proper.* The unqualified term 'psyche,' on the other hand, is used less restrictively by Jung: both the spheres of instinct and spirit can be considered 'psychic' in a looser, more general sense.

Which, of course, immediately raises the following questions: In what sense are instinct and spirit still *psychic*, given that they transcend deliberate personal volition? What does the qualifier 'psychic' refer to in such cases? I shall shortly address these questions but, for now, please bear with me a little longer.

Because the psyche proper is characterized by deliberate choice, it must entail a choosing *subject* capable of deliberation. In Jung's words, when it comes to

considered "choice" and "decision" which are peculiar to the will ... one cannot very well get round the need for a controlling subject (ONP: 98)

Therefore, the psyche proper is the *subjective* psyche, whereas the instinctual and spiritual domains are encompassed in what Jung interchangeably calls the *'objective* psyche' or the *'unconscious.'* The qualifier 'objective' is meant to highlight that processes in that part of the psyche (a) escape the control of our deliberate volition and (b) are common to multiple individuals, like shared instincts (cf. e.g. PR: 3-4); they are seemingly autonomous, animated by their own impetus, unfolding on their own accord whether we like it or not, and seem to be separate from us.[2] The term 'unconscious,' in turn, is meant to highlight that at least some of the defining properties Jung attributes to conscious contents—such as being accessible through introspection, as I shall soon discuss—are *not* present in the so-called unconscious.

Although the objective processes in the unconscious escape our introspective awareness and volitional control, we can still experience their *effects* on the subjective psyche, such as dreams, mystical visions, spiritual callings, sexual libido, etc. We cannot control these visions, callings and impulses, but we surely *experience* them from the position of *witness* or—on a more negative note—*victim* (cf. e.g. PR: 4 & 14). The objective, autonomous activity of the unconscious *impinges* on our subjective field of awareness, leaving a recognizable *imprint* on it. This is analogous to how physical processes in the outside world impinge and leave recognizable imprints on our sense organs.[3]

As we've seen above, for Jung the psyche *proper* is identical with consciousness (cf. ONP: 111). So we need to understand what exactly he means by 'consciousness,' if we are to grasp the nature of the psyche.

In modern philosophy of mind, the term 'consciousness' is usually understood in terms of what Ned Block (1995) called 'phenomenal consciousness.' Phenomenally conscious states are *experiential* in nature—i.e. states in which there is something it feels like to be. For instance, there is something it feels like to have a bellyache, to see the redness of an apple, to fall in love, to smell coffee, etc. Therefore, all these states are phenomenally conscious. As such, phenomenal consciousness— or, more simply, 'phenomenality'—entails *qualities of experience*, which may be perceptual (such as color, flavor, aroma, etc.) or endogenous (such as fear, love, desire, disappointment, etc.).

However, Jung defines 'consciousness' in a much more specific and restrictive manner. For him, consciousness is a relatively small *subset* of phenomenality, defined on the basis of three key properties. The first we have already encountered when discussing the psyche proper: only mental states under the control of *deliberate personal volition* are conscious. But then Jung adds:

because of its empirical freedom of choice, the will needs a

supraordinate authority, something like a *consciousness of itself*
... Volition presupposes a choosing subject who *envisages different possibilities*. (ONP: 110, emphasis added)

This is an allusion to what modern psychology calls 'meta-consciousness' (Schooler 2002) or 'self-reflection.' The "supraordinate authority" is a meta-cognitive experiential process that inspects, interprets and evaluates other, lower-level experiences corresponding to the "different possibilities" in question. In order to make a "considered choice" of one of these possibilities, the meta-cognitive process must *re-represent* the respective lower-level contents of experience. Jonathan Schooler explains:

Periodically *attention* is directed towards explicitly assessing the contents of experience. The resulting *meta-consciousness* involves an explicit *re-representation* of [phenomenal] consciousness in which one interprets, describes, or otherwise characterizes the state of one's mind. (Schooler 2002: 339-340, emphasis added)

By re-representing its own experiential contents—each re-representation constituting a *reflection* of an experiential content at a higher-level of cognition—the "supraordinate authority" achieves a kind of "consciousness of itself," as claimed by Jung.[4]

Jung seems to have searched for better ways to make this point throughout his career. Earlier writings show his struggle to convey his intuition clearly. For instance, in the passage quoted below he appeals to 'intensity,' 'concentration' and *attention* (just as Schooler does in the quote above) to allude rather cumbersomely to self-reflection:

While consciousness is intensive and concentrated, it is transient and is directed upon ... the *immediate field of attention*;

... matters stand very differently with the unconscious. It is not concentrated and intensive, but shades into obscurity; (MMSS: 190, emphasis added)

Be that as it may, the point is that consciousness entails a re-representation of psychic contents within the field of the subject's attention.

Here is a simple example to illustrate all this: suppose that someone asks you whether you feel pain in your belly. The question prompts you to introspect and evaluate your subjective field of bodily sensations by scanning it with your attention. In order for you to report that you do feel the pain, *two* conditions must be satisfied: first, you need to be *experiencing* the pain; second, you need to know *that* you are experiencing pain. This second condition—the knowledge *of* an experience—is the *re-representation*: a meta-cognitive *reflection* of a lower-level experiential content. Failing either condition, you cannot report the pain; not even to yourself.

Notice that the second condition is neither entailed nor implied by the first. Instead, it requires an *extra* experiential process in addition to the original experience. If you have the pain but don't become self-reflectively aware of it—by e.g. simply not paying attention to it—you won't know *that* you have it. For all practical purposes, everything will unfold as if you didn't have the pain.

Another example: although you always experience your breathing—the air flowing in and out of your nostrils, the movements of your diaphragm, the inflation and deflation of your lungs—only occasionally (such as right now, because I am bringing your attention to it) do you re-represent this experience and know *that* you have it. This ordinary and ubiquitous situation shows how easy it is for us to have experiences that we aren't self-reflectively aware of. And although it is simple for us to refocus our attention and re-represent the experience of breathing upon being prompted, other types of experience aren't re-representable even upon prompting (cf. e.g. Tsuchiya *et al.* 2015).

Therefore, re-representation or reflection is the mechanism by means of which consciousness amplifies or increases the 'intensity,' 'concentration' or clarity—better yet, *lucidity*—of some psychic contents. In Jung's words, "It is in the nature of the conscious mind to concentrate on relatively few contents and to *raise them to the highest pitch of clarity*" (ACU: 162, emphasis added). Not only is this what sets humans apart from the rest of nature, it is also what confers, in some important sense, *reality* to nature itself, for "without *conscious reflection* [the world] would not be" (MDR: 371, emphasis added).

In a clinical context, psychologists in Jung's time could not differentiate between the absence of an experience and the absence of the mere *re-representation* of the experience. In both cases, patients would not report the experience (not even to themselves). Only since recently—thanks to advances in neuroimaging and the development of so-called "no report paradigms" (Tsuchiya *et al.* 2015, Vandenbroucke *et al.* 2014)— can neuroscientists tell the difference. Therefore, it is perfectly understandable that Jung considers meta-cognition a necessary attribute of consciousness. After all, all he had to go with were the introspective reports of his patients.

Finally, Jung adds a *third* defining property of consciousness. While discussing the progressive development of awareness in children, he says:

> when the child recognizes someone or something—when he "knows" a person or a thing—then we feel that the child has *consciousness.* ... But what is recognition or knowledge in this sense? We speak of "knowing" something when we succeed in *linking a new perception to an already established context* ... "Knowing" is based, therefore, upon a conscious *connection*

between psychic contents. (MMSS: 100, emphasis added)

Ignoring the circular manner in which Jung seems to define consciousness in this passage, the key point is this: there cannot be consciousness without "firmly-knit" (ONP: 118) *webs of cognitive associations.* A child recognizes e.g. their mother because there are multiple cognitive associations linking 'mother' with other experiential contents, such as 'being cared for' (mother is a caretaker), 'home where I live' (which is where mother also lives), 'father' (man who is married to mother), 'car' (mother drives child to school), 'garden' (mother likes to spend time there), 'safety' (mother makes child feel safe), etc. For Jung, without these firmly-knit webs of associations there isn't really consciousness, for the latter entails the ability to place an experience in a broader cognitive context.

In summary, according to Jung consciousness is a subset of what we today call 'phenomenal consciousness.' In addition to being experiential in nature, conscious contents must:

(a) fall under the control of deliberate personal volition;
(b) be meta-cognitively re-represented or reflected, so as to be introspectively accessible and reportable; and
(c) be linked within a firmly-knit web of cognitive associations.

Henceforth, I shall consistently use the term 'consciousness' and the qualifier 'conscious' in the restrictive sense defined by Jung, and 'phenomenality' or 'experience' — along with the respective qualifiers 'phenomenal' and 'experiential' — when I mean the broader notion of phenomenal consciousness defined by Block (1995).

And now we are finally able to return to the questions raised earlier: In what sense are unconscious psychic contents still, well, *psychic*? What does the qualifier 'psychic' mean in the absence of consciousness?

As discussed earlier, the activity of the unconscious *directly impinges* on the psyche *proper*, in the sense that we can introspectively access its *effects* without mediation by the sense organs. So the unconscious and the psyche proper must, to some degree, overlap or 'touch' each other, which suggests that they are merely different regions of the same psychic ground. In Jung's words, the unconscious "has according to its effects a psychical nature" (JWL: 83)—i.e. it must have the same essence as that which it directly affects.

Moreover, there is also *traffic of contents* between consciousness and the unconscious. Conscious contents may fall into the unconscious upon being repressed or forgotten, while some unconscious contents may rise to consciousness in the form of erupting memories, insights, feelings and spontaneous behaviors. Assuming that the respective contents don't magically change their essential nature upon moving across the boundary, this traffic allows us to introspectively assert the psychic nature of (former or future) *un*conscious contents.

It is such empirically verified, unmediated interactions between consciousness and the unconscious—in the form of traffic and impingement—that motivate Jung to consider the latter an integral part of the psyche. Consciousness and the unconscious must both be *psychic*; they must have the same metaphysical ground or categorical basis, the difference between them being merely the relative strength of particular properties—namely, self-reflection, volitional control and cognitive association—of the respective contents.

Now, we've seen earlier that consciousness is a subset of the psyche's phenomenality. If so, it follows that the unconscious must also be essentially *phenomenal*, thus consisting of whatever phenomenality is *left* in the psyche *after* we've accounted for consciousness. In other words, unconscious contents must be *experiences* with a relative lack of volitional control, re-representation and cognitive association. Commerce of contents between the unconscious and consciousness is possible because these properties can strengthen or weaken over time for any given experiential content—i.e. cognitive associations can form and dissolve over time, contents can enter and leave the field of attention. Unconscious contents can directly impinge on consciousness because even qualitatively different experiences in the same psyche can impinge on one another: think of the last time your thoughts affected your emotions, or the other way around.

The essence of both consciousness and the unconscious is thus experiential, experience being the unifying factor that brings them together as integral parts of the psyche. There is no categorical transition between the two domains. In Jung's implicit metaphysical system, experience is what defines the nature of the psyche as a whole. Therefore, to say that something is psychic means to assert its intrinsically experiential nature, whether it's also conscious or not. The unconscious is psychic because it is experiential.

Such conclusion is both suggested and implied in Jung's work in a manner that renders it inevitable. There is just no other coherent way to construe the meaning Jung attributes to the qualifier 'psychic.' He consistently uses the term as an appeal to experience, mentation, such as when he claims that "the unconscious is psychical i.e. *a sort of mind*" (JWL: 83, emphasis added). At one point he even explicitly asserts the experiential nature—but lack of re-representation and introspective accessibility, respectively—of the unconscious by saying that it consists of "*experiences* that are either *unknown* or *barely accessible*" (PA: 3, emphasis added; see also p. 6).

Let us briefly recapitulate the discussion thus far. The psyche is defined by *phenomenality*: all its contents have an experiential essence or nature. Some of these contents are *conscious* in that they are controlled by deliberate volition, accessible through self-reflective introspection and linked in a web of cognitive associations. The remaining contents are *unconscious*. These unconscious contents are *objective* in the sense of being autonomous from the point of view of consciousness. The activity of consciousness and the unconscious can impinge on each other. When the unconscious impinges on consciousness, we experience the resulting effects in the form of dreams, visions and compulsive feelings. Some experiential contents can also move between consciousness and the unconscious, betraying the common metaphysical nature of these two psychic segments.

Jung goes out of his way to emphasize that the distinction between consciousness and the unconscious is a *relative* one. Taking the degree of self-reflection of a psychic content as a guide, he explains that consciousness

> embraces ... a whole *scale of intensities* of consciousness. Between "I do this" and "I am conscious *of* doing this" there is a world of difference. ... there is a consciousness in which unconsciousness predominates, as well as a consciousness in which *self-consciousness* predominates. (ONP: 115, emphasis added)

This unambiguous denial of any discontinuity between consciousness and the unconscious removes any doubt that, for Jung, both segments of the psyche are *essentially* of the same nature. The difference between them is merely one of degree. In the following passage, for instance, Jung refers to the relatively high degree of, respectively, self-reflection and association found in consciousness as its key differentiating properties:

> On a somewhat more primitive human level, ... consciousness ... ceases to be *reflected*. ... Here, as on the infantile level, consciousness is not a unity, being as yet uncentred by a *firmly-knit* ego-complex (ONP: 117-118, emphasis added)

By losing some of its associative links and capacity for self-reflection, consciousness starts to become more like the archaic unconscious.

The understanding that both consciousness and the unconscious are *experiential* in nature—the difference between them being merely relative, defined by the respective degrees of volitional control, self-reflection and cognitive association—is explicitly revealed when Jung talks, for instance, of "the conscious part of the experience" (PR: 48), which implies an experiential unconscious part. Without such understanding, certain passages of Jung's would sound preposterous. For instance, he maintains that

> never yet has any reasonable person doubted the existence of psychic processes in a dog, although no dog has, to our knowledge, ever expressed consciousness of its psychic contents. (ONP: 98)

Here Jung isn't denying that a dog has phenomenal inner life; much to the contrary: he is stating precisely that "no reasonable person" would doubt that a dog indeed *has* inner experiences—i.e. "psychic processes." But the dog lacks the depth of self-reflective introspection that allows humans to "express consciousness" *of* their experiences.

Moreover, when he says that "we can observe small children in the process of *becoming* conscious" (MMSS: 100, emphasis added), Jung obviously doesn't mean that babies and toddlers are zombies devoid of inner experience; he means solely that deliberate volition, self-reflection and associative links develop over time, in degrees. This is why "Every parent can see [this development], if he pays attention" (MMSS: 100).

Finally, when relating a near-death experience he had in 1944, Jung writes, "In a state of *unconsciousness*, I *experienced* deliriums and visions" (MDR: 320, emphasis added). Clearly, unconsciousness—in Jung's definition—is not incompatible with experience. This is why he can coherently claim that "The dream occurs when *consciousness* and will are to a great extent *extinguished*" (PR: 31, emphasis added), even though dreams obviously *are* experienced. What characterizes a state as unconscious—be it through syncope or mere sleep—is, in both these cases, a significant reduction in the degree of *meta*-consciousness. Indeed, modern studies have shown that meta-consciousness is greatly reduced during dreams (cf. Windt & Metzinger 2007).

Woven within the firmly-knit web of associations that characterizes our ordinary state of consciousness is a narrative of self-identity that Jung calls the 'ego'; a self-told inner story about who or what we are. As such, the ego is both a *content* of our ordinary consciousness and its *center*: because we identify with the ego, the other contents of consciousness seem to unfold around the ego just as our world seems to unfold around us (cf. MMSS: 101). For these reasons, Jung refers to our ordinary consciousness as 'ego-consciousness.'

Although some authors claim that 'ego' and 'consciousness' are synonymous in Jungian psychology, I beg to differ. The ego is the center of a *particular* web of experiential contents: namely, the one that populates our ordinary waking state. But we know that the psyche can seemingly break up into multiple, disjoint—yet internally connected—webs of conscious contents. This phenomenon is called 'dissociation' and, in recent years, its existence has been objectively demonstrated through modern neuroimaging methods (e.g. Schlumpf *et al.* 2014, Strasburger &

Waldvogel 2015). Dissociation can thus create split-off centers of experience inaccessible to ego-consciousness because of the absence of adequate associative bridges. Jung was not only aware of it, but also highlighted and elaborated on it rather extensively (cf. e.g. ONP: 98-104 & 118-130).

The result is that, unbeknownst to us—i.e. to our *ego-consciousness*—other centers of experience may inhabit our psyche along with us. Each of these hidden centers may entail a (deliberating) subject of experience. As such, they may be *conscious from their own perspective*, their respective experiential contents meeting the criteria for consciousness discussed earlier (although perhaps to a lower degree than ego-consciousness). Indeed, in a 1947 letter to Rev. Fr. Victor White, Jung clarifies that the contents of the unconscious may be in every sense indiscernible from the contents of ego-consciousness, except in that the former are not linked to—and thereby accessible from—the ego by appropriate associative bridges:

> the unconscious ... is not associated to Ego-consciousness, which is precisely the reason, why it is "unconscious." Though it might be conscious to another subject, an alter Ego, it is at all events severed from the Ego. (JWL: 83)

This is the second sense in which Jung talks of the unconscious as being *relative*: some unconscious processes may be unconscious *only from the perspective of ego-consciousness*, in that the ego cannot access them through introspection. But from their own perspective they may be (somewhat) conscious. To avoid confusion, each time I henceforth refer to the 'unconscious' I shall mean all experiential contents that are unconscious *from the perspective of ego-consciousness*.

Jung is quite explicit about all this. He claims that the unconscious may comprise psychic contents experienced by "a second consciousness" (ONP: 116). There may even be multiple ones of such fragmentary hidden subjects (cf. ONP: 118-130). Jung also acknowledges that assigning a subject to the unconscious effectively means "to lodge a consciousness in the unconscious" (ONP: 98), which he thinks empirical observations force us to do anyway, given "the cases of double personality, *automatisme ambulatoire* [dissociative fugue], etc." (ONP: 113). Because of the potential for secondary, fragmentary centers of consciousness, it is possible that "everything goes on functioning in the unconscious state just as though it were conscious" (ONP: 113).

However, while opening the door to these hidden centers, Jung is also quick to note that the unconscious *as a whole* "is not a second personality with organized and centralized functions but in all probability a decentralized congeries of psychic processes" (ACU: 278). In other words, the unconscious is not a single firmly-knit web of psychic contents, but instead comprises a number of relatively small webs connected, at best, loosely with each other. Therefore, he "would hardly venture to assume that there is in the unconscious a ruling principle analogous to the ego" (ACU: 276).

Yet *within* the "decentralized congeries of psychic processes" there may be *islands of consciousness* (cf. e.g. MMSS: 100, ONP: 118, PR: 102), disjoint but internally connected webs of experiential contents with some level of volitional control and re-representation. Jung often refers to these islands as the "multiple luminosities of the unconscious," which he defines as "'conscious-like' nuclei of volitional acts" (JWL: 54). He adds: "we would do well to think of ego-consciousness as being *surrounded* by a multitude of little luminosities" (ONP: 118, emphasis added).

This conjecture—as usual with Jung—is motivated by empirical observations:

although a "second ego" cannot be discovered (except in

the rare cases of dual personality), the manifestations of the unconscious do at least show *traces of personalities*. A simple example is the dream, where a number of real or imaginary people represent the dream-thoughts. In nearly all the important types of dissociation, the manifestations of the unconscious assume a strikingly personal form. (ACU: 283, original emphasis)

Each of these somewhat personified centers of consciousness remains nonetheless dissociated from ego-consciousness because the latter "cannot accept it for lack of understanding" (ONP: 100). In other words, the psychic contents in these islands of consciousness may be so alien, incongruent and incommensurable with the culture-bound references, logic and categories of ego-consciousness that they are shut out by the ego. Instead of being integrated into ego-consciousness, only their *effects* on ego-consciousness are explicitly cognized.

The implications of this view are profound. Jung is basically arguing that, in addition to non-re-represented, autonomous and cognitively isolated phenomenality, the unconscious may also comprise a veritable *population of somewhat conscious agencies distinct from the ego*, each with its own experiential contents. And since unconscious activity can impinge on ego-consciousness, these agencies can presumably *communicate* with the ego, as it were, through e.g. dreams and visions. Indeed, in Jung's view the psyche may be an *ecosystem* of communicating conscious agencies, in which ego-consciousness is merely one of the participants.

Chapter 3

Archetypes

[T]he world has been framed in the likeness of that which is apprehended by reason and mind and is unchangeable, and must therefore of necessity, if this is admitted, be a copy of something. ... [The universe can be thus divided into two classes:] one, which we assumed, was a pattern intelligible and always the same; and the second was only the imitation of the pattern, generated and visible. [T]he forms which enter into and go out of [nature] are the likenesses of real existences modelled after their patterns in wonderful and inexplicable manner ... [These real existences are] self-existent ideas unperceived by sense, and apprehended only by the mind.

Plato, in *Timaeus* (circa 360 B.C.E.)

As we've seen thus far, for Jung the unconscious comprises:

(a) relatively autonomous—'objective'—experiences outside the control of deliberate personal volition;

(b) experiences that, relative to consciousness, lack re-representation and, therefore, are at least less easily accessible through self-reflective introspection;

(c) experiences that, relative to consciousness, lack cognitive associations and, therefore, can't be placed in as wide a cognitive context; and

(d) somewhat *conscious* experiences belonging to internally connected webs of associations, such webs being, however, *dissociated from ego-consciousness.*

Some of these experiences in the unconscious can potentially cross the boundary and enter ego-consciousness, whereas others are fundamentally incapable of ever doing so. These latter experiences are what Jung refers to as *'psychoid'*—'almost psychic' or 'psychic-like'—contents, as opposed to fully psychic contents (cf. ONP: 110-111).

The reason for this distinction is easy to see. As discussed earlier, Jung has two motivations for considering the unconscious integral to the psyche: one is that unconscious processes can directly impinge on ego-consciousness and thereby produce introspectively discernible *effects*; the other is that at least *some* unconscious contents can altogether *cross into* ego-consciousness and be directly inspected. However, if other contents of the unconscious can *never* cross into ego-consciousness, we lose the latter motivation and cannot be as confident about their psychic nature.

Indeed, it is impossible for ego-consciousness to make definitive statements about the nature of contents that it can *never* inspect directly. In Jung's words, "Psychic existence can be recognized only by the presence of contents that are *capable of consciousness*" (ACU: 4, original emphasis). Therefore, Jung prefers the less metaphysically committal term 'psychoid' for experiential contents that never come under the microscope of the ego. These psychoid contents are 'almost psychic' or 'psychic-like' in the sense that they can still impinge on ego-consciousness without mediation and produce discernible effects. Beyond that, we cannot be absolutely sure about their essential nature.

Nonetheless, the kinship he intuits between these contents and truly psychic contents is so strong that—despite the conceptual inconsistency this leads to—Jung opts to consider the psychoid an integral part of the unconscious: "We must also *include in the unconscious the psychoid functions* that are not capable of consciousness"(ONP: 113, emphasis added).

The inconsistency is clear: contents that ostensibly *aren't* necessarily psychic—but *psychoid* instead—are integral to the unconscious. But since "the psyche is a conscious-unconscious whole" (ONP: 131), the unconscious—along with the psychoid—is integral to the psyche! So is the psychoid realm psychic or not? Is it essentially *experiential*, like the rest of the psyche, or something altogether different, despite its ability to interact *directly*—i.e. without mediation by the sense organs—with ego-consciousness?

It is easy to see, when perusing his work, that Jung consistently assumes the psychoid to be experiential, *psychic*, even though he makes an overt effort—at least when he's being careful—to remain uncommitted and leave the door open to alternatives. He does so simply because he can't defend this position on *empirical* grounds. Instead, he tries to project metaphysical agnosticism. Nonetheless, insofar as an implicit philosophical system can be attributed to Jung, such system would collapse if the psychoid weren't actually—like the rest of the psyche—just psychic. This will become clear later in this book.

Unlike Freud, Jung sees the unconscious as an *active* and *creative* agency in its own right, not merely a passive repository of repressed or discarded contents of ego-consciousness. As a matter of fact, Jung maintains that consciousness evolved *from* the unconscious, the latter being older (cf. e.g. ACU: 281, ONP: 92, MMSS: 191, MDR: 380-381). The idea is that consciousness is merely a later 'configuration' of the unconscious, featuring higher degrees of certain properties.

So for Jung *consciousness rests on the unconscious*, not the other way around. The latter is the original psyche, the root from which consciousness *grew* over time as the properties of volitional control, self-reflective introspective access and cognitive association slowly arose in some originally unconscious contents. This implies, once again, that the unconscious and consciousness have the same essential nature, in the same way that a flower has the same vegetable nature of the plant that produces it. Moreover, "Throughout life the ego is sustained on this base" (MDR: 382): the background activity of the unconscious continuously influences and organizes the foreground activity of consciousness.

Perhaps even more importantly, Jung posits that the foundations of the unconscious are *collective and transpersonal,* as opposed to being confined to any individual psyche. As such, the unconscious can be divided into two segments: the *personal* unconscious—which, like consciousness, is bound to a particular individual—and the *collective* unconscious. The latter is the foundational segment, older in an evolutionary sense and shared by all human beings. It is also the *psychoid* segment of the unconscious, in that its contents can never cross into ego-consciousness.

The structure and contents of the collective unconscious are *a priori*: they predate the rise of both consciousness and the personal unconscious and are independent of conscious experiences. The personal unconscious, on the other hand, corresponds more or less to the Freudian unconscious, consisting of dissociated, repressed, forgotten or otherwise discarded contents that originated in ego-consciousness, and which can return to ego-consciousness under appropriate conditions (cf. ACU: 3-4).

The picture we are left with is that of a psyche divided into three layers: the bottom, primordial layer is the collective unconscious, which consists of psychoid contents that can never reach ego-consciousness (although they can still *impinge* on ego-consciousness and thereby cause introspectively accessible *effects*, such as dreams and visions). The middle layer, sandwiched between the other two, is the personal unconscious. The top layer, which we ordinarily identify with, is ego-consciousness. Psychic contents can move between the personal unconscious and ego-consciousness.

The structure of the collective unconscious is defined by what Jung calls the 'archetypes.' These are primordial, *a priori templates* of psychic activity. To the degree that they escape the full control of deliberate volition, our emotions, beliefs, thoughts and behaviors unfold according to patterns that mirror these inborn archetypal templates. In two particularly eloquent passages, Jung describes the archetypes as

unconscious but nonetheless active-living dispositions, *ideas in the Platonic sense*, that preform and continually influence our thoughts and feelings and actions. (ACU: 79, emphasis added)

These "ideas in the Platonic sense" have

effects which have an *organizing* influence on the contents of consciousness. (ONP: 165, original emphasis)

For instance, the inner life and behavior of a mother towards her child is largely determined by the so-called 'mother archetype,' a mode of being and acting that is inherited by every woman and triggered—or 'constellated,' as Jung prefers to say—by the presence of her child (cf. ACU: 81-84). The inner life and behavior of many ambitious business leaders is largely determined by the so-called 'hero archetype,' a template for being and acting that, when constellated by external circumstances, steers and molds their thoughts, beliefs, emotions and behavior (cf. e.g. Campbell 2008). And so on. Each typical, spontaneous pattern of behavior, feeling, thought and belief in human beings is determined by an archetype. As such, according to Jung these patterns aren't learned but, instead, *inborn*; they correspond to the primordial templates of the collective unconscious as they assert themselves by impinging on ego-consciousness.

The basic idea here is that, insofar as we fail to deliberately assume volitional control of our inner life and behaviors, they *tend* to unfold along archetypal lines. These lines are innate dispositions of the psyche, which operate and exert their influence from outside ego-consciousness. From this background position they stimulate, steer and mold our conscious inner life and behaviors whenever they are constellated by the circumstances of the world around us. As our common inheritance, they largely define our humanity.

Clearly, the archetypes are intimately related to the instincts, in that they drive, regulate and modify contents of consciousness (cf. ONP: 136). One could say, for instance, that the patterns of being and acting of a mother towards her child are *instinctual*. As such, what we call 'instincts' can be looked upon as a *mode of expression* of the archetypes.

By the same token, what Jung calls 'spirit'—discussed earlier—is also intimately related to the archetypes:

> the archetypes have, when they appear, a distinctly numinous character which can only be described as "spiritual." (ONP: 136)

Spirit, therefore, can be regarded as another mode of expression of the archetypes.

In Jung's own words, instinct ("the biological pattern of behavior") and spirit ("the mythological archetype") are *"modos agendi,"* ways of acting of the archetypes (JWL: 70). It is the tension between the 'low,' egotistic energy of instinct on the one hand and the 'high,' impersonal energy of spirit on the other that fuels psychic life and creates its dynamisms (cf. ONP: 138-139).

Importantly, remember that Jung acknowledges the possibility that secondary centers of *consciousness*—to some degree self-reflective and deliberate, but relatively fragmentary and at any rate dissociated from ego-consciousness—populate the unconscious as subliminal agencies with their own resolve. This provides an explanatory basis for the 'daemons,' spiritual forces capable of imposing their impersonal agenda on ego-consciousness. Daemons can reside in the collective unconscious and act according to archetypal patterns, in a sense being *personifications of the archetypes*. Jung:

> the archetypes of the collective unconscious ... are to be regarded not only as objects [of the *objective* psyche] *but as subjects* with laws of their own. ... we have to admit that they possess spontaneity and purposiveness, or a kind of consciousness and free will. (AJ: *xv*, emphasis added)

Precisely for this reason,

> It not infrequently happens that the archetype appears in the form of a *spirit* in dreams ... Often it drives with unexampled passion and remorseless logic towards its goal and draws the subject under its spell (ONP: 137, emphasis added)

This way, the events of our conscious inner life may result not only from psychic dynamisms we consider our own, but also the actions of other agencies in the depths of the collective unconscious. Their activity impinges on our subjective field of experiences, attempting to shape the patterns of our thinking, feeling, believing and acting according to the archetypal templates they embody. The daemons *pull* ego-consciousness along a teleological path oriented towards the future achievement of psychic wholeness (cf. ONP: 141). I shall elaborate more on this later.

But first, an important distinction needs to be made: the archetypes themselves are *purely formal* and cannot be apprehended in and of themselves (cf. ONP: 146-147). They have an "organizing influence on the contents of consciousness" but can never themselves be directly accessed. All we can access is their *effects* on the organization of conscious contents, such as the archetypal patterns discernible in dreams and visions. These are *images* that result from conscious contents 'filling in' —like dough in a mold—*a priori* archetypal templates. As such, we only know that the archetypes exist because of the images they imprint on ego-consciousness.

Jung explains this by comparing an archetype

to the axial system of a crystal, which, as it were, preforms the crystalline structure in the mother liquid, although it has no material existence of its own. ... The archetype in itself is empty and purely formal (ACU: 79)

As such, insofar as we can know them, the archetypes are defined but abstract, have form but no content, just as the crystal's lattice structure before the crystal actually forms. They are *tendencies, dispositions,* even *probabilities*—as Jung posits when attempting to link the archetypes to the nondeterministic behavior of nature at a quantum scale (cf. AA: 70)—not experiences in and of themselves. Indeed, one could liken the archetypes to the intrinsic natural modes of excitation of a structure: they are the patterns according to which the psyche as a whole—as determined mostly by the structure of the foundational collective unconscious— naturally tends to 'move,' 'vibrate,' behave or express itself, because of what it intrinsically is. This is analogous to how a guitar string naturally tends to vibrate according to a certain note and not others, given its effective length and elasticity. Just as the notes produced by guitar strings exist only abstractly, in pure potentiality, unless and until the string is actually plucked, the natural, archetypal modes of excitation of the psyche are only discernible in actual experience, not in and of themselves.

Like a transparent stencil template, it is only when we 'fill it in' with conscious contents that the pre-existing form of an archetype becomes recognizable. The resulting archetypal image is a symbol that points to the *meaning* conveyed by the archetype, given the context within which it manifests itself. For instance, if one dreams of being in the arms of a female presence larger than life, a Jungian analyst could interpret it as a manifestation of the mother archetype, which could mean—depending on the concomitant situation in the dreamer's waking life—that the dreamer lacks and misses nurturing links, be it with others, with themselves or with the Earth. This is so because, according to Jung, dreams often have a compensatory function whose purpose is to balance out the various archetypal influences in our lives (cf. e.g. D: 40-41, PA: 46).

Another example: if an ambitious executive consistently displays compulsive patterns of behavior associated with the achievement of business goals, this could be construed as 'possession' by the hero archetype. Whereas the manifestation of this archetype is important in the transition from childhood to adulthood—wherein one must sever a relationship of dependency towards one's parents and childhood home—its continuing dominance hampers growth; it fixes an adolescent pattern of behavior whereby one forfeits recognition of one's own limits. In the dreams of a male executive overwhelmed by the heroic theme, other complementary archetypes—such as that of the wise old man (cf. A: 22)—may manifest themselves so as to facilitate psychic balance. The associated dream imagery must then be adequately interpreted so that ego-consciousness can heed its *message*—i.e. the meaning conveyed by the archetype—and recalibrate its attitude in waking life.

Each archetype can manifest itself according to a variety of images, feelings and spontaneous behavioral patterns, all of which symbolize—or point to—a message. Our deeper dreams, visions, passions and impulsive actions thus have a *meaning* and can be *interpreted*, if only we pay attention to them. Taken together, the archetypal manifestations in our lives—in both dream and waking states—form a symbolic narrative meant to show to ego-consciousness what is going on in the unconscious. They illustrate, in symbolic form, the longings, fears and insights of the unconscious, which remain dissociated from ego-consciousness or beyond the reach of self-reflective introspection. Importantly, they also illustrate *how the unconscious regards what is going on in ego-consciousness*, thereby conveying the unconscious's own perspective on life. Archetypal images thus represent an effort by the unconscious to *reach out* to ego-consciousness through impinging on the latter's subjective field. They are attempts at communicating with the ego, so that both segments of the psyche can work together in tandem.

In order to more concretely grasp how archetypal manifestations work and how they can constitute a symbolic message meant for ego-consciousness, consider the following interpretation of a deeply archetypal dream. The dreamer in question is my girlfriend and life partner. The dream occurred in the spring of 2015. She describes it thus:

I remember being chased by a huge mud monster that came to the shore from the sea. It ate everything in its path: bushes, plants and would eventually eat all humanity, because it was heading inland. My colleagues and I managed to run and find shelter in some sort of laboratory, where we would be temporarily out of the path of the monster. While in the lab, I was supposed to take a test (as in a school test), but I had to choose the test myself. I assumed that the more exciting and difficult the chosen test was, the higher the grade could be. I found an interesting crossword puzzle with images, but I thought it would be too easy and not the type of test I was expected to choose. At some point, I dropped the test and left the safe zone of the laboratory, moving to another, non-secure area that was in the path of the monster. I did it because I wanted to save a child who was left there, in harm's way. There was a constant feeling of fear, despair and hopelessness.

The muddy creature comes from the depths of the sea, which is a symbol of the collective unconscious (cf. ACU: 18): a deep, vast but hidden—'submerged'—region of the psyche, common to all humanity. For coming across as a monster, the creature represents a voracious, amoral, instinctual aspect of ourselves. Its muddy character evokes something dark but intimately linked to the ground, to the earth, to nature in its most raw and undomesticated form. The monster is thus an image of the *collective shadow archetype*: the instinctual, unthinking drives— greed, envy, aggression—intrinsic to our common humanity, but which we, as 'civilized' people, don't want to acknowledge.

The land—a visible region illuminated by the sun, which is a symbol of consciousness (cf. e.g. PA: 186)—represents ego-consciousness. When the monster was still hidden in the sea, not only was the dreamer's ego unaware of its existence, it also felt safe. But by leaving the sea and coming onshore, the monster invades consciousness and becomes recognizable, thereby threatening not only the dreamer, but also all humanity. *"There was a constant feeling of fear, despair and hopelessness,"* she says. The dream's message here is that the dreamer must become—or is slowly becoming—aware of the innate destructive potential of humanity, of which the dreamer herself is a member.

The monster *"ate everything in its path."* This is an evocative reference to humanity's compulsive, addictive, unthinking extraction and consumption of resources for egotistic short-term satisfaction, as well as of the environmental destruction they leave on their wake. As a creature of the unconscious, the monster is insatiable and never gives any consideration to—i.e. it doesn't *reflect* on—what it is doing. It is interested only in fulfilling its primal desires, which is symbolized by its eating voraciously. As the shadow of humanity, the monster embodies our behavior towards the Earth and its ultimate consequences for ourselves. The dream seems to be unambiguous on this point: *"eventually all humanity"* will be consumed.

But the dreamer's ego finds refuge in a laboratory, a symbol of the *reflective, rational, sensible* mode of operation of the psyche that, as such, insulates the personality from the domination of primitive drives and instincts; it constitutes a secure zone temporally out of the destructive path of the monster. The lab is also a place where research—inquiry, investigation—is done. This suggests that, from the perspective of the collective unconscious, humanity still has time and opportunity—through diligent self-inquiry—to bring its own shadow side under the lens of self-reflective examination and realize the insanity of its ways. There is still time for us to recognize our drives and compulsions for what they are, assume deliberate volitional control of them, and ultimately adjust our behavior before the destruction is complete and irreversible.

The dreamer starts a test, presumably for admission as permanent staff member of the laboratory. This symbolically suggests that her dispassionate reasoning faculties—and, by implication, those of all humanity—can permanently balance out her instincts, provided that she overcomes a certain barrier or challenge. But she has the freedom to choose the test herself, so presumably she can pass simply by choosing a test she finds easy. The suggestion is that everyone is qualified to do the necessary self-inquiry, provided that one does it in harmony with one's own natural dispositions and abilities. That the dreamer felt she had to choose an *"exciting and difficult"* test betrays her ego's need to fulfill artificial expectations from others, instead of simply focusing on what she can naturally— and therefore effortlessly—do. The unconscious sees these mistakes and, through the dream, tries to express its point of view to the dreamer's ego. Perhaps the barrier or challenge to be overcome is in the *choice*—not the *passing*—of the test: Does our ego give us the opportunity to express ourselves according to the natural dispositions and abilities of our *whole* psyche? Or does it, instead, restrict us to the confines of our ego's arbitrary, culture-bound notions of self-worth?

However, before the dreamer can finish the test, she feels an irresistible urge to save a child who is in harm's way, despite having to risk her own life in the process. This may symbolize the complementary paths of living from the head (finishing the test, doing research and staying safe) and living from the heart (surrendering to empathy and the thoughtless, spiritual expression of compassion when the situation calls for it, despite the risks). The path of the heart sometimes allows the collective unconscious to express its balancing archetypal influence almost directly.

Moreover, the child in the dream is likely an image imprinted by the child archetype, the universal template of growth and future realization of intrinsic potentials (cf. ACU: 151-181). The fact that the child is in a *"non-secure area"* outside the lab means that, although we can ensure our short-term safety by thinking things through and staying within our intellectual comfort zone, our future development may nonetheless require taking perceived emotional risks. Be that as it may, the dreamer's choice is clear: through the spontaneous, spiritual expression of empathy and compassion, she presumably saves the child and safeguards her—and, symbolically, humanity's—potential for growth and future development. As stated in the Talmud, "whoever saves a single life is considered by Scripture to have saved the whole world."[5]

The tension between instinct and spirit is palpable in the dream, fueling the amazing richness of the dreamer's psychic life. The ability of the unconscious—the dream-maker—to weave such an evocative symbolic narrative, entailing multiple, simultaneous, intertwined layers of meaning, is uncanny. Its imagery isn't literal, but instead points to something beyond itself. In other words, the imagery *means* something other than its face-value appearances, which can only be grasped through the pursuit of a chain of feeling-toned cognitive associations.

By leveraging innate associative links — such as those between the image of a child and growth potential, a devouring monster and instinctual greed, the seashore and the border between ego-consciousness and the unconscious, a mother figure and nurturing relationships, etc. — the archetypes evoke meaning through a *universal* language accessible to all humans, independently of cultural background. In doing so, they impulsively seek to steer us towards the achievement of the ultimate psychic goal.

That ultimate telos or goal of psychic life is, according to Jung, 'individuation' (cf. ACU: 275-289): a full realization of the whole personality in conscious awareness. Each archetype embodies a part of the personality's latent potential, all of which seek expression and recognition in consciousness. In other words, the psyche seeks to develop the properties of volitional control, self-reflection and cognitive association for all its contents, so they can be — indirectly, in the case of psychoid contents — examined and deliberately integrated into a harmonious whole. The manifestations of the archetypes in our lives — whether in dreams, visions or instinctual feelings and behaviors — aim precisely at advancing the psyche towards this teleological destination. They point to a preferred developmental direction. Therefore, according to Jung, attention must be paid to the *meaning* of archetypal manifestations, if we are to succeed in the process of individuation and achieve the ultimate psychic objective. The unconscious provides the clues, but ego-consciousness must deliberately *reflect* on their symbolic connotations and grasp the message.

Jung explains all this in a wonderfully eloquent passage:

All these moments in the individual's life, when the universal laws of human fate [i.e. the archetypes] break in upon the purposes, expectations, and opinions of the personal consciousness, are stations along the road of the individuation process. This process is, in effect, the spontaneous realization of the whole man. The ego-conscious personality is only a part of the whole man, and its life does not yet represent his total life. ... since everything living strives for wholeness, the inevitable one-sidedness of our conscious life is continually being corrected and compensated by the *universal human being in us,* whose goal is the *ultimate integration of conscious and unconscious,* or better, the assimilation of the ego to a *wider personality.* (D: 80, emphasis added)

Figure 1 depicts Jung's map of the psyche, summarizing everything discussed thus far. In the figure, ego-consciousness is shown surrounded by the unconscious. From the left, ego-consciousness is influenced by the instincts, one mode of expression of the archetypes in the collective unconscious. From the right, the spirit, another mode of expression of the archetypes, influences it. The tension between these two opposing influences is what powers the dynamisms of psychic life. The spirit may also comprise daemons: secondary, possibly fragmentary centers of consciousness—at any rate dissociated from ego-consciousness—that impinge on the subjective

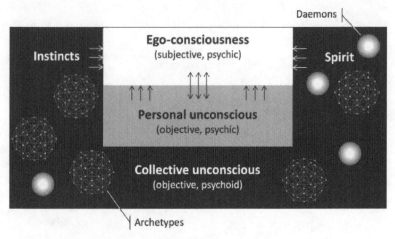

Figure 1. The map of the psyche according to Jung.

field of introspectively-accessible experiences. The personal unconscious underlies ego-consciousness, not only influencing it but also exchanging contents with it. The ultimate goal of psychic life is to expose to the light of consciousness—i.e. to cognitively connected, deliberate, self-reflective introspection— every aspect of the psyche, either directly or through their effects on ego-consciousness, so the psyche can meta-cognitively know itself fully.

Chapter 4

Synchronicity

Cause and effect—"Explanation" is what we call it, but it is
"description" that distinguishes us from older stages of knowledge
and science. Our descriptions are better—we do not explain any
more than our predecessors. … we infer: first, this and that has
to precede in order that this or that may then follow—but this
does not involve any comprehension. … Cause and effect: such a
duality probably never exists; … An intellect that could see cause
and effect as a continuum and a flux and not, as we do, in terms
of an arbitrary division and dismemberment, would repudiate the
concept of cause and effect and deny all conditionality.
Friedrich Nietzsche, in *The Gay Science* (1882)

Jung's notion of 'synchronicity' is crucial to his metaphysical
views, in that *synchronicity transcends the boundaries of psychology*
and makes statements about the physical world at large. Its key claim
is that, in addition to chains of cause and effect, the physical
world organizes itself also according to *archetypally determined*
relationships of meaning, like dreams do, as we've just seen.

Jung contrasts synchronicity with mechanistic causality so to
highlight why the latter isn't sufficient to account for how we
relate to the physical world and—even more importantly—how
the physical world relates back to us. So let us start by reviewing
the notion of causality.

David Hume considered causality "the cement of the universe,"
in that physical events hang together through chains of cause
and effect. Whatever happens in the physical universe—except
perhaps the primordial creation event, the Big Bang itself—has
a cause and an effect, even if the latter is not noticeable. It is by

virtue of these chains of cause and effect that the configuration of the physical world changes and evolves through time.

Philosophers still debate what causality is. Much of that debate, however, consists of hair-splitting efforts to correctly define causality in words, even though we intuitively know what we mean by it. It is thus safe to ignore the philosophical details and concentrate only on a couple of salient points.

We acquire our understanding of causality through observing the *regularities* of nature's behavior. In other words, our notion of causality is—at least largely—empirically derived. For instance, we may observe that when a first, moving billiard ball hits a second, resting one, the latter begins to move. In fact, this happens every time we see a moving ball hit a static one, so we come to expect it and eventually even take it for granted. It is these repeated, consistent observations that motivate us to abstract a corresponding causal regularity: a moving body *causes* a static body to move if and when they collide. More generally, by observing nature's patterns of behavior carefully, we can progressively catalog their various regularities, which then provide a foundation for our understanding of causality.

However, regularities alone aren't sufficient. For instance, a storm regularly follows a falling barometer, yet that doesn't mean that the falling barometer *causes* the storm. As a matter of fact, it is a reduction in atmospheric pressure that causes *both* the falling barometer *and* the arrival of the storm. Moreover, sometimes an observed regularity is merely a coincidence, implying no causal connection between events. For instance, "Miss Unsinkable" Violet Constance Jessop was onboard the *Titanic*, the *Olympic* and the *Britannic* when disaster struck all three ships. But that doesn't mean that the presence of Ms. Jessop *caused* ship disasters.

So philosophers have devised an additional criterion for identifying causality: *counterfactual dependence*. The idea is simple: suppose that an event *B* regularly follows an event *A*.

We want to know whether *A causes B*, whether perhaps *A* and *B* are both caused by a third event, or whether the observed regularity is merely coincidental. To figure this out we set up an experiment under controlled conditions, wherein we first induce *A* and then check whether *B* follows. *Ex hypothesi, B* will follow. Then we repeat the experiment by ensuring that every salient condition is replicated, *except that this time around we don't allow A to happen*. Does *B* then *still* occur? If it doesn't, then we can be more confident that *A* indeed causes *B* for, everything else being sufficiently the same, *B* doesn't occur in the absence of *A*. Technically, we say that *B* is 'counterfactually dependent' on *A*.

Together, regularities and counterfactual dependencies provide a practical basis for identifying causal relationships in nature.

Regularities and counterfactual dependencies are *observable physical phenomena*, empirically accessible to us. If we simply look around, and maybe set up some experiments, they obligingly reveal themselves. Yet, what we call 'causality' is not these physical observables themselves, but that which *underlies* and *explains* them—i.e. that which, from behind the scenes, makes them unfold the way they do. As such, causality is a *meta*physical organizing principle underlying, and immanent in, physical nature. The scientific models—theories—we mathematically articulate and refine over time are just *approximations* of this underlying organizing principle. Without postulating such metaphysical ground, we would be forced to regard regularities and counterfactual dependencies as arbitrary flukes, mere artifacts of chance, for there would be no *a priori* reason for them to happen.

Allow me to belabor this a bit more for clarity: what we *do* observe empirically are the *results* of the action of an inferred, underlying causal principle that, in and of itself, remains invisible to us. We don't see causality; we only see its manifest consequences in nature's behavior. Therefore, the underlying organizing principle is *meta*physical, instead of physical. It is derived on the basis of *induction*—the theoretical inference of a general law from repeated instances of conjoint events—which goes beyond empirical observation. Presumably because of his close collaboration with Nobel Prize-winning physicist Wolfgang Pauli, Jung follows most physicists in attributing to this metaphysical organizing principle the character of *law* (cf. AA: 7). Accordingly, he regards the relationship between cause and effect as one of *necessity*, as opposed to e.g. merely habitual. In other words, specific effects *must always* result from their corresponding causes, for such consistency is metaphysically dictated. Jung is quite explicit in this regard: "The causality principle asserts that the connection between cause and effect is a *necessary* one" (S: 95, emphasis added), he says.

The level of applicability of this necessity, however, depends on whether we take a *macro*scopic or a *micro*scopic perspective. From the macroscopic perspective of e.g. Newtonian mechanics, cause and effect are linked through an exchange of energy or momentum and the associated necessity applies to *single events*: each and every effect will *deterministically* result from its cause, according to the corresponding Newtonian law. From the truer, microscopic perspective of quantum mechanics, however, cause and effect are linked through an exchange of field quanta and the associated necessity applies *only at a statistical level*: individual quantum events unfold seemingly randomly but, when taken together in large numbers, the events lawfully comply with predictable probabilistic distributions.

The scientific consensus today—as well as in Jung's time—is that classical, macroscopic physics arises as the compound result of fundamental microscopic (quantum) laws, only the latter being metaphysically real. In the words of physicist Erich Joos, simply to assume, or rather postulate, that quantum theory is only a theory of micro-objects, whereas in the macroscopic realm per decree (or should I say wishful thinking?) a classical description has to be valid ... leads to the endlessly discussed paradoxes of quantum theory. These paradoxes only arise because *this particular approach is conceptually inconsistent* ... In addition, micro- and macro-objects are so strongly dynamically coupled that we do not even know where the boundary between the two supposed realms could possibly be found. For these reasons it seems obvious that *there is no boundary*. (Joos 2006: 74-75, emphasis added)

Joos goes on to state, "whichever interpretation [of quantum mechanics] one prefers, the classical world view has been ruled out" (2006: 76). Therefore, Newtonian mechanics is merely a handy *approximation* of quantum mechanics for systems comprising a very large number of particles. In these macroscopic systems, the inherent indeterminacy of quantum mechanics averages itself out and neatly translates into mostly predictable behavior because of the large number of microscopic events involved.

And here is the opportunity Jung (and Pauli) spotted: strictly speaking, there is a non-zero chance that a billiard ball will behave *differently* than predicted by Newton's laws. For instance, there is a non-zero chance that a static billiard ball will move on its own — in a non-causal or 'acausal' manner — without being hit by another ball. It's just that this chance is vanishingly small.

In the simple case of billiard balls, any acausal event would jump out to even casual observation and freak us out. But in complex chaotic systems, such as our everyday physical environment, it is conceivable that small, acausal quantum fluctuations could translate inconspicuously into significant macroscopic events — think of the so-called 'butterfly effect.'[6]

For being rooted in rolls of the quantum dice, these macroscopic events would, strictly speaking, *lack a cause*. Yet we would be none the wiser about it, for the complexity of our physical environment is just too great for us to keep tabs on its causal chains anyway. We would just *assume* that the acausal event in fact *had* a cause, but one too impractical to trace back.

As a matter of fact, cosmology today states that tiny, acausal quantum fluctuations in the early universe are what led—after amplification by gravity—to the formation of everything, from microbial life to galaxies (Lloyd 2006: 48-51). In the words of Seth Lloyd,

> Counterintuitive as it may seem, quantum mechanics produces detail and structure because it is inherently uncertain. ... Every galaxy, star, and planet owes its mass and position to quantum accidents[7] of the early universe. But there's more: these accidents are also the source of the universe's minute details. ... Every roll of the quantum dice injects a few more bits of detail into the world. As these details accumulate, they form the seeds of all the variety of the universe. Every tree, branch, leaf, cell and strand of DNA owes its particular form to some past toss of the quantum dice. (Lloyd 2006: 49-50)

When studied individually, subatomic particles behave seemingly randomly, like dice. Yet it is conceivable that, in complex systems encompassing many particles, individual quantum events at the single-particle level could be aligned with each other according to some *global* pattern, spanning across many particles. Let me illustrate this with a simple analogy.

Imagine that you toss three dice on a table, multiple times. After each toss, you inspect each die separately and verify that they randomly display a number from one to six. But when you look at all three dice together, you realize that either they *all* display an even number or they *all* display an odd number. The resulting *global pattern* not only clearly violates randomness, but is also constituted by individual events that, when inspected in isolation, meet randomness criteria.

Indeed, the possibility of there being a global synchronization mechanism in nature is opened up by quantum mechanics itself:

> Because of the non-local properties of quantum states, a consistent description of some phenomenon in quantum terms must finally include the entire universe (Joos 2006: 71).

That being said, even if they are common in nature, it is impossible for physicists to identify global alignments across quantum events. For although physicists can test individual events in the laboratory and verify that, when taken in isolation, the events are random, they wouldn't be able to discern a *global* pattern within the complexity of the physical world at large; there are just too many 'dice' to keep track of under controlled laboratory conditions.

Many physicists thus simply *assume* that the quantum fluctuations at the foundation of our physical environment do not follow any global pattern. But since complex systems are impractical to study at the quantum level, we can't run a randomness test on their compound quantum behavior to confirm it (cf. Kastrup 2011: 34-38). For all we know, instead of accidents, quantum events conform to subtle, non-local patterns of organization corresponding to a yet-unacknowledged metaphysical ordering principle, different from causality.

This is what Jung bets on. Perhaps the structure of the entire universe—from galaxies to strands of DNA—which we today attribute to mere chance, arose in fact as a result of such unrecognized global patterns.

Indeed, it is both conceivable and physically coherent that, unbeknownst to us, acausal macroscopic events are still regularly happening around us. As put by Mile Gu *et al.,*

The question of whether some macroscopic laws may be fundamental statements about nature or may be deduced from some [microscopic] 'theory of everything' remains a topic of debate among scientists. (Gu *et al.* 2009: 835)

If there are such irreducible macroscopic patterns, they—unlike cause and effect—may not entail relationships of strict necessity, but tendencies, affinities or dispositions instead. Therefore, as Jung stresses (cf. S: 2), we cannot expect to pin down the corresponding events on the basis of empirical regularities and counterfactual dependences. Not only may these events not be consistently repeatable, the global patterns they reflect may be excluded from experiments by our very efforts to isolate the experimental setup and control its conditions. We cannot induce these acausal events at will. The best we can do is to pay attention to the world around us, in the hope of noticing one of them as it spontaneously unfolds.

It is precisely this open space for a yet-unrecognized metaphysical organizing principle—operating at a global, macroscopic level—that Jung seizes and populates with his ideas. According to him, next to causality, the physical world organizes itself along *archetypal correspondences of meaning*, which break down the barrier between world and psyche. As Jung puts it, "Within the randomness of the throwing of the dice, a 'psychic' orderedness comes into being" (AA: 62).

I shall elaborate on this shortly but, for now, the key question that arises is: Why does Jung feel the need to propose a new metaphysical organizing principle to begin with? Why isn't causality enough?

Jung reports an incident he once witnessed during a therapy session with a female patient. The patient was relating a dream in which she was given a golden scarab, an important archetypal symbol of re-birth. As she was recounting the dream, an insect began knocking against the window behind Jung. He opened the window and a rose chafer beetle—an insect very much like a scarab—flew in. It was as if the *physical world itself* were echoing the archetypal symbolism of the dream the patient was recounting (cf. S: 33).

Elsewhere Jung discusses the 'unidentified flying objects' (UFO) phenomenon (FS). He points out that the human psyche is by nature split between opposing tendencies—instinct and spirit—and, therefore, under significant tension. Sometimes this tension triggers an attempt by the psyche to heal itself. The archetype of the self—representing the union of opposites, wholeness—is then constellated in the witness's psyche, while a coincidental *physical* event occurs in the sky outside. This external event—whatever it may be—often entails an object with round or cylindrical form, which is also a symbol of wholeness (cf. FS: 111).

Further examples of such *meaningful coincidences*—i.e. conjunctions of an inner psychic state with an external physical event, both of which share the same archetypal meaning—are mentioned in Jung's works (cf. e.g. S: 20-40). In the case of the scarab event, the shared meaning was re-birth. In the case of the UFO reports, it was wholeness.

In all these examples, it is inconceivable that the psychic state and the external event could have been brought together by virtue of a causal link. For instance, it is inconceivable—on the basis of our scientific understanding of causality—that the recounting of the patient's dream could have *caused* the arrival of the beetle, or the other way around. It is equally inconceivable that a third, unknown event could have caused both the patient's dream and the arrival of the beetle. After all, what exchange of field quanta could possibly have resulted in both events? Therefore, as Jung is at pains to point out (cf. S: 11-12), we must discard causality as the ordering principle behind such meaningful coincidences.

Which leaves us with mere chance. In principle, it is coherent to imagine that the conjunction of the dream recounting and the beetle's arrival was purely accidental. However, for Jung, two arguments render such hypothesis dissatisfying: the specificity and affective force of the *meaning* evoked by the coinciding events, and the sheer *unlikelihood* of such conjunctions happening merely by chance.

Indeed, for reasons I shall soon illustrate, Jung includes parapsychological phenomena—such as clairvoyance—in the category of meaningful coincidences. He then cites contemporary experimental results that produced high odds against chance for these phenomena (cf. S: 22-27). Jung leverages such results to argue that, statistically speaking, meaningful coincidences cannot be mere flukes. They must, instead, be orchestrated by a yet-unrecognized organizing principle in nature. While resting his case largely on the experimental confirmation of parapsychological phenomena, Jung also seeks to provide a plausible mechanism for how and why these phenomena may occur.

Today, based on the latest research, we know that parapsychological phenomena are indeed most likely real (cf. Cardeña 2018). But against this, we must also weigh the more sophisticated understanding we now have of the psychological mechanisms underlying the experience of coincidences, such as cognitive bias and contextual dependence (cf. Elk, Friston & Bekkering 2016). In other words, the affective force of meaningful coincidences, which Jung partly relies on, may often rest on illusion.

And here, although I could conveniently follow the standard protocol and hide behind a façade of scholarly detachment, I would like to express my personal view. After all, what could be more appropriate in a book about Jung's work, given that he insists we shouldn't dismiss our personal experiences in favor of any abstract, statistical truth (cf. US: 1-12)? So, although I do believe that many—even most—experiences of meaningful coincidence are illusory, being mediated by relatively prosaic psychological mechanisms, my own experiences make it very difficult for me to dismiss Jung's case. In the course of my life, the archetypal meaning occasionally evoked by events in the world around me—in precise alignment with my own inner state, or that of someone close to me—has been just too compelling to attribute to chance or cognitive bias.

I shall relate only two illustrative examples. A few years ago, I was on vacation with my girlfriend in a small village in the German countryside. We had been out of touch with friends and family for about a week at that point. One morning my girlfriend woke up and immediately told me a dream she had just had, and which for some reason had made an unusually strong emotional impression on her. In the dream, her old grandmother—who, in real life, was alive and well last time we had been in touch— appeared with a bandage of gauze wrapped around her head. She was in a hospital, flanked by two of her daughters (my girlfriend's aunts). None of the three said a word, although my girlfriend felt distinctly that her grandmother was telling her, mentally, that she was still okay, despite the head injury.

We thought we should call my girlfriend's father and inquire about her grandmother, just in case. And so we did. The first thing her father said was that his mother—i.e. my girlfriend's grandmother—had just had a *brain stroke* and was *hospitalized*. *Two of her daughters were with her* in the hospital. The first medical assessment was that *she wasn't in immediate danger anymore*. Yet, as it turns out, she would die six months later of directly related causes.

My girlfriend's grandmother was the most important source of feminine, grounded, earthly wisdom in my girlfriend's life. She embodied the archetype of the wise old woman. The three women in the dream together formed a triad, another archetypal image. And, of course, the theme of approaching death is also profoundly archetypal.

So my girlfriend's inner psychic state that morning—colored by layers of archetypal undercurrents as it was—coincided very meaningfully with an actual state of the outside world, which in turn reflected back those same archetypal themes. If I hadn't witnessed this in real-time, as the events unfolded, I probably would have been skeptical. But there I was, confronted with a textbook instance of a meaningful coincidence, presented to me in a way that I couldn't dismiss.

The other example is more recent and—appropriately enough—directly related to the writing of this book. As I was working on the manuscript and doing research on Jung, I found myself on the shores of Lake Constance, not far from Jung's birthplace. I was reminiscing about the fact that he felt attracted to water since childhood, thanks to his early exposure to the very lake in whose waters I now had my feet immersed. I then spontaneously recalled a story he tells in his autobiography: to facilitate contact with the unconscious, he used to give free rein to his imagination and build little houses, castles and even whole villages with pebbles from the lakeshore where he lived. Once he built a little church but missed a suitable pebble to play the role of altar. He then chanced upon a reddish, four-sided, pyramid-like pebble on the shore—about an inch and a half (four centimeters) high—and immediately knew that it was the appropriate piece (cf. MDR: 198).

As this reminiscence unfolded in my mind, a very quick succession of spontaneous cognitive associations—pebbles, lakeshore, my feet in the water—automatically made me look down. Bizarrely, right there, just in front of my feet and about eight inches (twenty centimeters) under water, was a *reddish, four-sided, pyramid-shaped pebble*, unambiguously fitting Jung's description. Having measured it a few days later, I discovered that it was—you guessed it—about an inch and a half high. See Figure 2.

Figure 2. The reddish pyramidal pebble I found in Lake Constance—
echoing Jung's own finding about a century earlier—photographed
immediately after I found it.

This finding was all the more remarkable to me because, when
I first read that passage of Jung's autobiography, I felt skeptical
of his description: a pyramid-shaped reddish stone fetched
from a lakeshore? I had never seen anything resembling such a
description and had trouble imagining that it could be accurate.
Red is an unusual color for a lake pebble. Moreover, what kind
of erosion could produce a four-sided pyramid shape anyway? I
ended up attributing the whole thing to poetic license and Jung's
fertile imagination. Nonetheless, I now had a pebble in my hands
that fit Jung's description uncannily accurately. It was as if the
physical world were conspiring to show me—through more
than one layer of meaning—that I should *never* be dismissive of
Jung; that I should *always* take him very seriously, despite my
prejudices and potentially skewed sense of plausibility.

My intellect—as is its habit—quickly ran through conventional explanations: maybe I had subliminally seen the pebble *first* and, only thereafter, thought of Jung's story because of a trivial association. But no, this couldn't have been the case: I had not been looking down but ahead, to the place where I knew Jung had been born. So I couldn't have seen the pebble first. Then I considered the possibility that such pyramid-shaped stones were common in the lake, in which case there would be nothing remarkable about my finding one in front of my feet. So I started diligently looking for other similar pebbles all around, but could find none. Insofar as I could ascertain, the stone I first found was quite unique, at least in that part of the lake.

This was another clear case of a meaningful coincidence, psychologically difficult to attribute to mere chance. In that sunny afternoon in Lake Constance, both my inner psychic state and the physical state of the world around me embodied and reflected the same archetypal content: a solid, pyramidal symbol of transcendence and timelessness, fished out of the waters of the unconscious.

But that isn't the end of the story. A few days later—the coincidence of the pyramidal pebble still reverberating in my mind—my girlfriend and I went hiking in a region of the world the young Jung considered magical: the Swiss Alps. One sunny afternoon we found ourselves entirely alone—except for a few marmots—in a desolate but magnificent alpine valley, well over a mile (two thousand meters) high. A stream ran through the valley's floor and, precisely in the middle of it, we came upon a large boulder—about three feet (a meter) high—almost perfectly shaped as a *four-sided pyramid*. Indeed, the pyramidal shape of the boulder was so perfect I needed to rely on my analytical judgment to convince myself of the impossibility of its having been deliberately sculpted and transported to such a remote place. Here was the physical world insisting even more loudly—as if the first time round hadn't been clear and persuasive enough—on its message. It was as if Jung's ghost were accompanying us. See Figure 3.

Figure 3. A naturally eroded pyramidal boulder in *Val Fedoz*, outside Sils-Maria, Oberengadin, Switzerland.

My invitation to you is thus this: consider Jung's case in light of your own personal experiences and intuitions. How do you feel about the hypothesis that there is another organizing principle in nature, next to mechanistic causality, associating the events of our lives according to their evoked meaning?

My girlfriend's dream about her grandmother could be interpreted both as an instance of clairvoyance and a meaningful coincidence. This equivalence is the reason why Jung bundles meaningful coincidences and parapsychological phenomena together in the same category. He calls this category—i.e. this additional organizing principle in nature—'*synchronicity,*' which he defines as the simultaneous occurrence of a certain psychic state with one or more external events which appear as meaningful parallels to the momentary subjective state (S: 36)

As such, synchronicity entails an equivalence of symbolic meaning between our inner psychic state and the concurrent physical state of the world surrounding us, as if they mirrored each other. This is metaphysically significant, for it abolishes the separation between world and psyche. Indeed, synchronicity suggests—if it doesn't outright imply—a unity between psyche and physics, something Jung makes a point to emphasize when he reviews other philosophical notions related to it (cf. S: 95-122). For instance, when discussing Chinese philosophy, Jung highlights that some sages "supposed that the *same* living reality was expressing itself in the *psychic* state as in the *physical*" (S: 51, emphasis added). In fact, in a letter to Pauli written on November 30, 1950, Jung is quite open about this possibility:

[A] synchronistic event can be described as a characteristic of the psyche or mass [i.e. matter]. In the former case, the psyche would cast a spell on mass, and in the latter mass would bewitch the psyche. It is thus more probable that both ... are basically contingent and, heedless of their own causal definitions, *actually overlap*. (AA: 62, emphasis added)

Jung's writings on synchronicity are peppered with subtle suggestions that this unifying metaphysical ground underlying both psyche and physics is *experiential*. For instance, when comparing the work of Wilhelm von Scholz to his own, Jung chooses to highlight that von Scholz

suspects that these [meaningfully coincidental] happenings are arranged as if they were the dream of a "greater and more comprehensive consciousness" (S: 22)

Jung seems to use strategically selected third-party quotations like this to plant a metaphysical idea in the mind of his reader, while circumventing the implication that he himself is in the business of metaphysics. The dilemma that forces him into such a roundabout strategy is that, whereas he insists that "Synchronicity is not a philosophical view but an empirical concept" (S: 133), without the planted metaphysical idea his next claim would be difficult to grasp: *"Meaningful coincidences ... seem to rest on an archetypal foundation"* (S: 34, emphasis added).

So just like our most significant dreams, in Jung's view the physical world itself is shaped—at least to some noticeable extent—according to archetypal templates, "which are psychic events *par excellence*" (MDR: 385, original emphasis). Events of the waking world around us are themselves woven along archetypal contours. In an important sense, what Jung is saying is that our physical, waking reality is amenable to symbolic interpretation, just as our dreams are. The external world, too, conveys meaning through symbolic expression, as if it were "the dream of a greater and more comprehensive consciousness."[8]

As we've seen earlier, the archetypes are *a priori*, fundamental templates of psychic activity that constitute or reflect the structure of the collective unconscious. By claiming that synchronicities unfold according to archetypal patterns, Jung is implying that the collective unconscious underlies both consciousness *and the physical world itself*. This is a remarkable claim, as it means that *physical events are orchestrated by the same a priori patterns that orchestrate events in consciousness*. Jung acknowledges this explicitly:

The archetype ... reveals itself to psychic introspection—so far as inward perception can grasp it at all—as an image, ... which underlies not only the psychic equivalences but, remarkably, *the psycho-physical equivalences too*. (S: 138, emphasis added)

This is so because

the archetypes are not found exclusively in the psychic sphere, but can occur just as much in circumstances that are not psychic (equivalence of outward physical process with a psychic one). (S: 137)

To drive this point home and eliminate any conceivable ambiguity, Jung says elsewhere:

It is perfectly possible, psychologically, for the unconscious or an archetype to take complete possession of a man and to determine his fate down to the smallest detail. At the same time objective, non-psychic parallel phenomena can occur which also represent the archetype. *It not only seems so, it simply is so, that the archetype fulfills itself not only psychically in the individual, but objectively outside the individual.* (AJ: 58, emphasis added)

An implication of this uncompromising claim is that the collective unconscious and the physical world are related in effectively the same way as the collective unconscious and ego-consciousness. And since Jung posits that ego-consciousness arises out of the unconscious, as a particular manifestation of it, it follows that the physical world itself must also arise from the collective unconscious, as another manifestation of it. If so, one must logically conclude that the physical world is as essentially *experiential* as the psyche.

For Jung, the collective unconscious underlies and permeates the whole of space in a non-local fashion. This means that the expression of the archetypes in the physical world is *global*, instead of being restricted by the locality constraints of causality, such as the speed of light limit. In other words, archetypal patterns organize the world *instantaneously across space,* operating within the degrees of freedom left open by the indeterminacy of quantum-level events. As Jung puts it,

> the central structure of the collective unconscious cannot be fixed locally but is an ubiquitous existence identical to itself; it must not be seen in spatial terms and consequently, when projected onto space, is to be found everywhere in that space. I even have the feeling that this peculiarity applies to time as well as space. (AA: 13)

There is thus a significant sense in which—if Jung is correct—the world surrounding you right now presents itself physically to you as an *integrated whole.* Moreover, *this whole has a message:* it is interpretable as "the dream of a greater and more comprehensive consciousness." Every bit of the physical world, across space and time, may express global archetypal meaning; it may be telling a story. From this perspective, it is entirely legitimate for you to ask yourself: What does the world around me mean? What does its imagery symbolically represent? *What is it saying?*

It is important to realize that, for the same reason that the scientific notion of laws of nature is metaphysical in character, Jung's synchronicity—an acausal ordering principle underlying, and immanent in, the physical world—has a metaphysical character as well. There is no doubt that Jung's motivation for postulating synchronicity is empirical (namely, the occurrence of seemingly meaningful coincidences), just as the motivation for postulating laws of nature through induction is also empirical (namely, the observation of regularities and counterfactual dependencies). Nonetheless, what is *entailed* by both postulates is inevitably metaphysical.

Moreover, one should *not* regard the archetype as the *cause* of synchronicities. That would bring us right back to, well, causality. The archetype is not a causal agency, but the *natural template* according to which both the human psyche and—if Jung is correct—the physical world *spontaneously* organize themselves. This is analogous to how the crystal spontaneously grows according to a particular, identifiable lattice structure, without the lattice itself constituting a causal agency.

As the growth of a crystal is ordered by an abstract lattice structure, the unfolding of both psyche and physical world are ordered according to archetypal patterns. Jung then further conjectures that *numbers* also have an archetypal foundation or character: they are archetypes of *order* (cf. S: 57-59). This conjecture—further elaborated upon by Jung's pupil, psychologist Marie-Louise von Franz, in 1974—allows us to solve a problem that only became widely acknowledged in the last year of Jung's life: the question of why and how mathematics models and predicts the *order* of the physical world so accurately and precisely.

Indeed, in 1960 physicist Eugene Wigner published a paper titled "The Unreasonable Effectiveness of Mathematics in the Natural Sciences." In it, Wigner discusses "the miracle of the appropriateness of the language of mathematics for the formulation of the laws of physics." To illustrate his point, he recounts an anecdote: a professor of statistics shows to a friend some graphs and equations that model human population trends. In one of the equations, the friend notices the symbol 'π' (pi) and asks what it is. The professor then explains that 'π' is the number you get when you divide the circumference of the circle by its diameter. The friend reacts with incredulity: "surely the population has nothing to do with the circumference of the circle." Yet, somehow it actually does.

This and other similar correspondences between abstract mathematics and concrete physical realities illustrate a seemingly extraordinary fact: concepts and logic axioms in the psyche—such as numbers and numerical operations—describe the physical world in unexpected but uncannily correct ways. Why should this be so? Why should the *physical* world comply with our *psychic* axioms? That it does is probably the reason why Wigner uses the word 'miracle' twelve times in his paper.

Now notice that, if numbers are archetypes of order underlying *both* human thinking *and* the physical world at large,

the possibility can be predicted that equations can be devised from purely mathematical prerequisites and that later they will turn out to be formulations of physical processes. (AA: 128)

Indeed, if the ordering principles or templates behind our mathematical reasoning are also behind the empirical order of the physical world, it should be no surprise at all that Jung's 'prediction' turns out to be precisely true. At the level of the collective unconscious, psyche and world are, *ex hypothesi*, continuous with one another. The same ordering archetypes—numbers and their associated operations—define the regularities of both.

On the one hand, Wigner's miracle can be construed to provide empirical substantiation to Jung's notion that archetypes—including numbers—extend into the world at large. On the other hand, the hypothesis of synchronicity makes *good sense* of Wigner's miracle. When Jung's far-reaching insights are liberated from the confined domain of the *human* psyche alone, the chain of implications and resulting explanatory synergies are extraordinary.

Jung and Pauli were keenly aware of how far the explanatory power of synchronicity could coherently be taken. In correspondence exchanged between November 1950 and February 1951 (cf. AA: 53-71), they discussed extending the concept of synchronicity to *all acausal events in nature*, not only those accompanied by a semantically equivalent psychic state. This needs some unpacking, so bear with me.

The human psyche operates largely through cognitive associations based on *similarity*. For instance, there is a famous painting by René Magritte wherein a pipe is depicted above the phrase *"Ceci n'est pas une pipe"* — French for "this is not a pipe." The pun is that the *painting* of a pipe is not the pipe itself. The latter is a three-dimensional wooden object, whereas the former is a two-dimensional pattern of pigment on canvas. Yet, there obviously is a certain *similarity* between the pipe and its depiction on canvas, which motivates us to casually look at the latter and declare that it *is* a pipe. *We cognitively associate the pipe and the painting on account of their cognitively salient similarities.*

More generally, we associate different psychic contents based on their similarities, this being perhaps the most innate form of associative logic in the psyche. For this reason, when two similar psychic events happen in conjunction — say, seeing a man with arms laterally outstretched and thinking of a cross — we are hardly surprised: they are cognitively associated because of what they have in common.

This notion of similarity should be interpreted here in the broadest sense, encompassing more than just direct correspondences of form. For instance, we naturally associate the image of a party balloon, the memory of a toy and the taste of cream frosting because, for many of us, they all evoke similar memories of childhood. Hence, what these things have in common — the basis for their association — is the similarity of what they *evoke*, not their particular form. Under this broad understanding, a correspondence of *meaning* is just an instance of *similarity*, so defined.

According to the definition of synchronicity we have been using thus far, what configures a meaningful coincidence is the conjunction of an *inner* psychic state with an *outer* physical event that are *similar* in the broad sense just discussed. This way, Jung extrapolates the innate psychic basis for an association between two psychic contents to a basis for an association between a psychic content and a *physical* event. But what about *two coincidental physical events*, without any psychic state to accompany them? Is the basis for such purely physical conjunction always causal, never synchronistic?

There is a problem with answering this question in the affirmative. You see, Jung finds room for synchronicities in the indeterminacy—the apparent randomness—of *individual* quantum events. In a synchronicity, these individual events aren't really random, but instead structured according to a non-local archetypal pattern. This doesn't violate any physical laws because the latter entail relationships of necessity only at a *statistical*—not an individual—level, encompassing many quantum events.

The problem is, if *some* individual quantum events follow global synchronistic patterns—being, therefore, structured according to such patterns—and others are really just random, we are left with an arguably arbitrary discontinuity in nature: Why should the *same kind of event*—namely, microscopic quantum events—sometimes be globally structured and sometimes not? If synchronicity is a universal, metaphysically real, immanent ordering principle, it should *always* apply, analogously to how the laws of nature are thought to always apply.

This is why Jung ultimately extends the definition of synchronicity as follows:

> Synchronicity could be understood as an *ordering system* by means of which "similar" things coincide, without there being any apparent "cause." (AA: 60, original emphasis)

Such definition accommodates the conjunction of two *similar*—in the broad sense discussed above—*physical events* as synchronistic, even in the absence of a corresponding psychic state.

Now, Jung—with the high-caliber support of Pauli (cf. AA: 65)—proposes that this broader notion of synchronicity is the ordering principle underlying *all acausal happenings* in nature (cf. S: 138-139, AA: 38 & 60). And since *no* individual quantum event is causally determined, the implication is that *all* quantum events, at a microscopic level, must be structured according to some global pattern of similarities. We don't ordinarily recognize this global pattern because its non-local character renders its repetition and study under controlled laboratory conditions impractical.

It follows from this that synchronicity—insofar as it defines the structures or tendencies underlying *all* quantum events—is *the only metaphysically real* ordering principle in nature. The laws of nature we are familiar with in our daily lives become mere epiphenomena of archetypal synchronicities, something Jung seems to realize when he observes that it is

> fundamentally impossible to prove that the law of nature is actually based on something *toto coelo* [i.e. totally] different from what we in psychology call archetype. (AA: 70)

Indeed, just as *macro*scopic events aren't fundamental, but the aggregate results of many *micro*scopic ones, under this broader view of synchronicity causality isn't a fundamental organizing principle either, but a regular compound outline of many microscopic synchronistic events. In other words, causality is to synchronicity as Newtonian mechanics is to quantum physics. Causal regularities are just *discernible local contours* of much more subtle, *global* patterns of similarity in nature. For Jung, ultimately everything in nature unfolds according to similarity-based associations.

Notice what he is doing: he is extrapolating the natural basis for cognitive associations *in the psyche* to a universal basis for the organization of *all events in nature*. He seems to regard the whole universe as a supraordinate cosmic mind—a "greater and more comprehensive consciousness"—operating on the principle of association by similarity, just as the human psyche does. As a matter of fact, as we shall see in the next chapter, this may be precisely what his metaphysical position entails.

Chapter 5

Metaphysics

The objective method can be developed most consistently and carried farthest when it appears as materialism proper. It regards matter, and with it time and space, as existing absolutely, and passes over the relation to the subject in which alone all this exists. Further, it lays hold of the law of causality as the guiding line on which it tries to progress, taking it to be a self-existing order or arrangement of things, veritas aeterna, *and consequently passing over the understanding, in which and for which alone causality is. ... Materialism is therefore the attempt to explain what is directly given to us from what is given indirectly. ...* [It] *is the philosophy of the subject who forgets himself in his calculations.*

Arthur Schopenhauer, in *The World as Will and Representation* (1818)

To discuss Jung's metaphysical views may at first seem inappropriate, as he repeatedly emphasizes that his work is an *empirical* endeavor, as opposed to philosophical or theological speculation. Jung consistently tries to project the image of a metaphysically agnostic *scientist* of the psyche, not a philosopher.

His writings contain clues to the motivations behind this attitude. For instance, Jung laments that many reject the hypothesis of an unconscious based merely on capricious theological or philosophical assumptions, apparently oblivious to the empirical evidence. He speaks of the need to replace a purely philosophical view of the psyche with one based on actual experience (cf. ONP: 81-90). This stance is best seen in a passage wherein Jung attempts to contrast an empirical view of the archetypes with a metaphysical one:

Were I a philosopher, I should continue in this Platonic strain and say: Somewhere, in "a place beyond the skies," there is a prototype or primordial image of the mother that is pre-existing and supraordinate to all phenomena in which the "maternal," in the broadest sense of the term, is manifest. But I am an empiricist, not a philosopher (ACU: 75)

Here Jung seems to be confessing to his covert metaphysical position: a Platonic view of the collective unconscious, according to which the archetypes are analogous to Plato's 'Ideas' — i.e. *actual transcendent entities in their own right,* metaphysically real and irreducible, underlying physical reality but not dependent on it for their existence. Yet, he stops short of acknowledging this view so as to emphasize the empirical basis of his psychology.

It is easy to see in his writings that Jung's perennial concern is to prevent his postulates from being rejected merely because, according to some metaphysical position such as materialism, they supposedly *can't* be true. In a 1945 letter to Fr. White, Jung is quite candid about this:

My temperamental empiricism has its reasons. ... My audience then [i.e. in the beginning of Jung's career] was a *thoroughly materialistic crowd,* and I would have defeated my own ends, if I had set out with a definite creed or with definite metaphysical assertions. I was not and I did not want to be anything else but one of them. ... [Therefore,] I have tried to accommodate myself to the psychiatric and medical mind. (JWL: 6, emphasis added)

So as to fit in, Jung decided to focus on empirical evidence, for the latter cannot be ignored on philosophical grounds. After all, philosophy must accommodate the evidence, not the other way around. This way, Jung hopes to insulate his work from philosophical fashions and ephemeral notions of plausibility or lack thereof—the "spirit of this time," as he originally put it (RB: 229-231). This becomes evident in the following passage:

> In former times ... it was not too difficult to understand Plato's conception of the Idea as *supraordinate* and *pre-existent* to all phenomena. *"Archetype" ... was synonymous with "Idea"* in the Platonic usage. ... It so happens—*by the merest accident, one might say*—that for the past two hundred years we have been living in an age in which it has become unpopular or even unintelligible to suppose that ideas could be anything but *nomina* [i.e. mere names or labels, not real existents]. (ACU: 76, emphasis added)

Notice how Jung seems, once again, to be confessing to his actual metaphysical position by suggesting that the archetypes are "real entities" in the sense of being "supraordinate and pre-existent to all phenomena." Indeed, looking upon the archetypes as equivalent to Plato's Ideas has major metaphysical implications, as Schopenhauer explained when framing his own concept of the 'will' in a similar fashion (Schopenhauer & Payne 1969): the equivalence turns physicality into mere and ephemeral *appearance*, while making of the archetypes (and the 'will') the invisible, eternal *inner essence* of all reality. Originating already with Parmenides, this division of nature into eternal essence and ephemeral appearance lies at the very root of Western philosophy and has been articulated again and again throughout history. To speak only of the period since the Enlightenment, Emanuel Swedenborg referred to the essence as 'spirit' and the appearance as 'correspondence'; Kant called them the 'noumenon' and the 'phenomenon,' respectively; Schopenhauer the 'will' and the 'representation'; even I speak of 'intrinsic view' and 'extrinsic appearance' (cf. Kastrup 2019). In likening the archetypes to Plato's Ideas, Jung thus seems to take the inner essence of everything—the true nature of the whole world, as it is in itself—to be *psychoid*, a major metaphysical step counter to the spirit of his time. This probably gave him pause and made him extra hesitant about acknowledging his philosophical inclinations.

Be that as it may, Jung's overt attitude towards philosophy seems to be based on a prejudice. He seems to think of philosophy as a discipline of ungrounded, idiosyncratic speculation, detached from the world of actual experience and empirical evidence. It's a view applicable perhaps to medieval scholasticism, in which philosophy and theology were intertwined and detached from concrete reality. However, it isn't consistent with philosophy as it has been practiced at least since the early 20th century.

When it comes to metaphysics, for instance, philosophers today tend to be keenly aware of the latest results from experimental science, for *interpreting* these results from a metaphysical perspective is precisely what their job entails. While science studies the *behavior* of nature, philosophers interpret this behavior so as to formulate hypotheses regarding what nature essentially *is*, in and of itself. Contrary to being a speculative alternative to science, philosophy—particularly metaphysics—in fact *complements* science. If Jung had had this understanding, he most likely wouldn't have publicly distanced himself from philosophy as much as he tried to, for his core ideas have profound philosophical implications.

As a matter of fact, ultimately he acknowledges as much:

I fancied I was working along the best scientific lines ... only to discover in the end that I had involved myself in a net of reflections which extend far beyond natural science and ramify into the fields of philosophy, theology, comparative religion, and the humane sciences (ONP: 149)

He even suggests that the crossing of the bridge linking psychology to philosophy is *inevitable*:

philosophy and psychology are linked by indissoluble bonds which are kept in being by the inter-relation of their subject-matters. ... Neither discipline can do without the other (MMSS: 183)

It is thus legitimate to investigate—as this book attempts to do—the metaphysical implications of Jung's propositions. By his own admission, his work has such implications. In addition, it is also legitimate to attempt to infer the metaphysical opinions Jung may have covertly held, yet stopped short of publicly declaring so as to maintain the politically-correct image of a metaphysically-agnostic scientist. After all, as he himself says,

Agnosticism maintains that it does not possess any knowledge of God or of anything metaphysical, overlooking the fact that one never *possesses* a metaphysical belief but is *possessed by* it. (AJ: 117, original emphasis)

As such, despite his repeated attempts to distance himself from metaphysics—of which he let go only in the last few years of his life, as discussed later in this book—there is plenty of evidence in the body of his technical work that Jung was, all along, "possessed by" certain metaphysical beliefs. What these beliefs entail will slowly come into focus as we make our way through the rest of this chapter.

To begin with, there is one *negative* metaphysical position that becomes clear very quickly as one peruses Jung's work: he repeatedly and unambiguously *rejects* mainstream metaphysical materialism, the notion that physicality is all there is, the psyche being an (emergent) epiphenomenon of brain metabolism—or at any rate *reducible* to the brain. Jung states this position very clearly and succinctly: "The psyche as such cannot be explained in terms of physiological chemistry" (ONP: 107). But he goes on to elaborate on it in several other passages. For instance:

> the psyche ... is existent but *not in physical form.* It is an almost ridiculous prejudice to assume that existence can only be physical. (PR: 11, emphasis added)

And:

> Despite the materialistic tendency to understand the psyche as a mere reflection or imprint of physical and chemical processes, there is not a single proof of this hypothesis. Quite the contrary, innumerable facts prove that the psyche translates physical processes into sequences of images which have hardly any recognizable connection with the objective [i.e. physical and chemical] process. The materialistic hypothesis is much too bold and flies in the face of experience with almost metaphysical presumption. (ACU: 57-58)

One might add, as an aside, that whatever level of presumption is involved here it is most certainly *metaphysical* presumption, for materialism is a metaphysical—not a scientific—hypothesis.[9]

As for the possibility that, in the absence of consciousness, psychic contents are merely physiological, Jung has this to say:

> except for the relation to the conscious ego, nothing is changed when a content becomes unconscious. For this reason I reject the view that momentarily unconscious contents are only physiological. ... the psychology of neurosis provides striking proofs to the contrary. (ONP: 113)

Remarkably, in his extensive refutation of materialism Jung even anticipates—by more than sixty years!—the recognition of what has only in the mid-nineties (Chalmers 1995) come into focus as the 'hard problem of consciousness':[10]

we have literally no idea of the way in which what is psychic [i.e. experiential] can arise from physical elements, and yet cannot deny the reality of psychic events (MMSS: 184)

As a matter of fact, Jung considers the denial of materialism one of the "basic postulates" of his psychology (MMSS: 177-199). In an extensive elaboration of the *subjective, psychological prejudices* motivating the onset of materialism—which he attributes to an overcompensation of medieval views that accounted for too much in terms of spirit (cf. MMSS: 182)—Jung categorically denies that materialism is justifiable by objective, rational reasons. He calls it an "irrational reversal of standpoint," an "unreasoned, not to say emotional, surrender to the all-importance of the physical world" (MMSS: 178)—i.e. he downright *psychologizes* materialism, something I've also attempted to do leveraging 21st-century psychological insights (Kastrup 2016b). And as if to preempt any conceivable doubt, Jung adds:

Let no one suppose that so radical a change in man's outlook [i.e. materialism] could be brought about by *reasoning and reflection*. ... [Instead, it] is a *mere trick* if we consider it as a question for the intellect (MMSS: 178-179, emphasis added)

For Jung, *both* the medieval spiritual view *and* the modern materialist view are unjustifiable extremes motivated by subjective biases; one shouldn't account for too much in terms of either matter or spirit, understood here as speculative metaphysical substrates distinct from the psychic. Instead, only the *psychic*—as the middle, epistemically reliable position—is solid ground, matter and spirit being each "a mere designation for the particular source of the psychic contents" (MMSS: 195). He develops his entire psychology on this basis, which Jungians to this day refer to as 'the reality of the psyche.'

Jung does acknowledge that at least some psychic functions are, in some way, closely related to parts of the nervous system (cf. ONP: 108). However, he accounts for this relationship in a surprising way:

> it is always the [psychic] function that *creates its own organ* [!], and maintains or modifies it. (ONP: 102-103, emphasis added)

Remarkably, here we have Jung completely inverting the logic of mainstream materialism: it's the psychic function that creates, maintains and modifies the organic structure, not the other way around. This is an extraordinary assertion that Jung, unfortunately, does not elaborate further upon. Nonetheless, it is not an isolated event in his corpus: in an earlier work, Jung echoes the same idea when claiming,

> We do not know whether there is a real disturbance of the organic processes of the brain in a case of neurosis, and if there are disorders of an endocrine [i.e. organic] nature it is impossible to say whether they are not *effects* rather than causes. (PR: 10, emphasis added)

Again, Jung inverts the logic of materialism by suggesting that an organic brain disorder may be the *effect*—not the cause—of a psychic condition. Indeed, this seems to be a position he held since the beginning of his career, for in an even earlier work Jung criticizes the mainstream view of the mind-body relationship in the following terms:

> Today the psyche does not build itself a body, but on the contrary, matter, by chemical action, produces the psyche. *This reversal of outlook would be ludicrous* if it were not one of the outstanding features of the spirit of the age. (MMSS: 180,

emphasis added)

He goes on to regret the mainstream view that it is

intellectually unjustified presumption on our forefathers'
part to assume that ... there is a power inherent in [the human
soul, i.e. psyche] which *builds up the body, supports its life, heals
its ills* (MMSS: 180, emphasis added)

The gist of Jung's view of the mind-body relationship is thus that
the body owes its existence and function to the psyche, not the
other way around. This reflects the epistemic and metaphysical
primacy that Jung consistently attributes to the psychic realm, as
we shall shortly see.

In contrast to his usual flirting with metaphysics, in the
correspondence he maintained with Pauli on the topic of
synchronicity Jung goes to unreasonable lengths—perhaps
because of Pauli's intimidating stature as a scientist—to
avoid metaphysical speculation and stick solely to what can
be *ascertained empirically*. In this spirit, at one point Jung even
claims that "metaphysical judgment ... always places an element
of the psychic in an external location" (AA: 100). In other words,
metaphysical judgment always entails *conceptual abstractions*
pointing beyond direct, personal empirical experience.
For instance, we cannot ascertain that matter outside and
independent of experience exists, for all we have are perceptual
experiences. Similarly, we cannot ascertain that a standalone
spiritual realm exists, for all we have are intuitive and visionary
experiences. So by postulating that the psyche is either material
or spiritual—both of which are metaphysical judgments—we
are placing the psyche itself on external, non-ascertainable
metaphysical ground.

Jung's point is that all we can ever ascertain is our own

introspectively accessible phenomenal inner life, everything else being theory. However, as strictly correct as this may be, unless one is prepared to adopt solipsism—the notion that only one's own *personal* experiences exist—and live accordingly, one cannot avoid metaphysical inferences of one sort or another. Even under idealism, one must metaphysically *extrapolate* the existence of experience beyond one's own personal boundaries, so to account for the phenomenal inner lives of other living beings and the universe at large (cf. e.g. Kastrup 2019).

As Bertrand Russell pointed out, solipsism "is psychologically impossible to believe, and is rejected in fact even by those who mean to accept it" (2009: 161). Were Jung a solipsist, it would be very difficult to understand why he is so interested in the supposedly non-existent inner lives of his patients. Therefore, despite his overt denials, Jung *must* make inferences beyond what can be directly ascertained empirically. Pauli confronts Jung on this point by observing that, if one is to pursue

the total elimination of everything from the interpretation of nature that is "*not* ascertainable *hic et nunc*" [i.e. here and now] ... then one soon sees that one does not understand anything—neither the fact that one has to assign a psyche to others (only one's own being ascertainable) nor the fact that different people are all talking about the same (physical) object ... one has to introduce some *structural elements of cosmic order, which "in themselves are not ascertainable."* (AA: 104, emphasis added)

It is ironic that, of all people, Pauli, a physicist, has to confront Jung with the inevitability of non-ascertainable metaphysical inferences.

Be that as it may, as already suggested in the previous chapter, the most significant metaphysical implication of Jung's views stems precisely from the theory of synchronicity, which he so carefully crafted with Pauli's assistance: by stating that the physical world arranges itself to symbolically *connote* something—*anything*, let alone archetypal meaning—Jung is saying that *psychic powers somehow control its behavior.* Otherwise, how could the physical world know how to express meaning, such quintessentially psychic aptitude?

Indeed, the expression of meaning through denotation or connotation always entails *cognitive associations*—i.e. semantic links between behaviors and the meaning they reflect, embody or are intended to evoke—and thus can only take place in the context of *cognition.* For instance, you only know to shake your head from side to side to express negation or disapproval because there is a cognitive association *in your psyche*—which underlies and is immanent in the behavior of your physical body— between the gesture and the ideas of negation and disapproval. In contrast, matter supposedly outside and independent of the psychic doesn't arrange itself to denote or connote anything; it purportedly just follows mechanistic causal laws. For Jung, thus, on some underlying and immanent metaphysical level, *there has to be a transpersonal psychic layer associated with the physical universe at large.* This layer must perform the cognitive associations necessary for the universe to express meaning through its behavior, in a way analogous to how you express meaning when you shake your head from side to side.

This, it seems to me, is an inevitable, inescapable implication of synchronicity. The physical world can only express meaning if psychic powers underlie and determine its behavior, such powers operating on the basis of semantic associations. As immediate, instinctual and spontaneous as such expression of meaning may be, it still presupposes an underlying psychic agency. There is just no way around it.

One approach to accommodate synchronicity metaphysically is to think in dualist terms. For instance, we could imagine that human beings have both a visible physical body and an underlying psyche of a non-physical nature—a soul—which controls the body from an invisible metaphysical background. By the same token, we could also postulate that there are both a visible physical world of matter and an underlying, non-physical, immanent universal mind that controls the world's behavior from an invisible metaphysical background. The question then is: Is such dualism consistent with Jung's larger body of ideas and positions?

I submit that it isn't.

Jung invites us to think of the psyche as something analogous to the spectrum of light, which runs from the infra-red to the ultra-violet. In the middle of the spectrum, corresponding to visible light, we have the psyche *proper*. On the higher, ultra-violet end we have the spiritual psychoid. On the lower, infra-red end we have the instinctual psychoid (cf. ONP: 143-144 & 146). As already discussed, the implication of this way of thinking is that there must be no difference *in essence* between the psychoid and the properly psychic, for the same reason that light across all colors of the spectrum, visible or otherwise, is still essentially *light*. The only difference between the properly psychic and the psychoid must thus be one of *degree*, just as red (or even infra-red) and violet (or even ultra-violet) light differ only in frequency of oscillation.

Crucially, Jung pushes the light spectrum analogy beyond the psychoid segments of the psyche and into the *physical and spiritual worlds at large*:

> Just as the "psychic infra-red," the biological instinctual psyche, *gradually passes over* into the physiology of the organism and thus *merges with its chemical and physical conditions,* so the "psychic ultra-violet" … describes a field which … can no longer be regarded as psychic, although it

manifests itself psychically. (ONP: 148-149, emphasis added)

Jung is suggesting here that the psyche—through its psychoid segments—"gradually passes over into" matter on the one end and spirit on the other. Such continuity between matter, psyche and spirit implies that there can be no fundamental metaphysical distinction between them. These three categories must, instead, represent but *relative differences in degree of manifestation of one and the same substrate.*

The passage above isn't an isolated fluke. Jung is perhaps even clearer about this point in another work:

> The unconscious is the psyche that *reaches down* from the daylight of mentally and morally lucid consciousness *into the nervous system* that for ages has been known as the "sympathetic." (ACU: 19, emphasis added)

His highlighting the label 'sympathetic' suggests that, in his view, the sympathetic nervous system has something to do with relating to someone else's inner feelings, as in sympathy, rapport or empathy. Indeed, Jung continues with yet another extraordinary claim, oozing with major metaphysical implications:

> [The sympathetic nervous system] not only gives us knowledge of the *innermost life of other beings* but also has an *inner effect upon them.* (ACU: 20, emphasis added)

Significantly, both the knowledge and the effect alluded to above take place without mediation by the senses, for—as Jung makes a point to emphasize—the sympathetic nervous system functions "without sense-organs" (ACU: 19). Moreover, reading this passage in its context, one can find no reason to interpret it as merely metaphorical. Instead, Jung seems to be stating, as plainly as it can be stated, that what we call the 'sympathetic nervous system' represents a *transpersonal metaphysical ground that psychically connects living beings together,* allowing them to directly exchange knowledge and psychic influences with one another. One can hardly avoid the conclusion that, with this claim, Jung is providing a metaphysical interpretation of the collective unconscious itself. The claim eliminates any possible categorical distinction between the psyche and the matter of the nervous system.

As a matter of fact, Jung explicitly acknowledges in a letter to Pauli that "the physical and psychic matrix is *identical"* (AA: 126, emphasis added). His motivation for saying so is the already discussed fact that, according to synchronicity theory, the archetypes organize the material world at large just as they organize the psyche proper. So it's difficult to imagine—if synchronicity holds—that matter and psyche could be essentially distinct. Instead, Jung posits that they have the same categorical basis.

But what about spirit? Is its categorical basis different from that of psyche and matter? After reminding Pauli that "Psyche is for me, as you know, a general term indicating the *'substance'* of all phenomena of the *inner world"* (AA: 125, emphasis added), Jung proceeds to contend that

> Spirit ... characterizes a specific category *of this substance—* namely, all those contents that cannot be derived either from the body or from the external world (AA: 125, emphasis added).

So not only are matter and psyche identical in essence, spirit and psyche are also essentially the same. And as if to nicely— though redundantly—complete this triangle of identities, Jung adds somewhere else:

Spirit and matter may well be forms of *one and the same transcendental being.* For instance the Tantrists, with as much right, say that matter is nothing other than the concreteness of God's *thoughts.* (ACU: 212, emphasis added)

Any conceivable doubt about these metaphysical identities is eliminated when Jung confirms that even the *psychoid* segment of the psyche is constituted by the common "substance": "Among the things that are part of the *substance* of the psychic are psychoid archetypes" (AA: 126, emphasis added).

Therefore, *matter, psyche (including the psychoid) and spirit are all manifestations of a single substrate;* they all share the same categorical basis; they are all constituted by the same intrinsic essence. Consequently, *there is no room left for dualism.* For Jung, there is no spirit separate from matter and no matter separate from psyche. Jung is, most definitely, a metaphysical monist.

But what, then, is this common essence? An important—perhaps even decisive—clue is given when Jung states that, in the interplay of psyche, matter and spirit, *"the psyche must be given a middle or superior position"* (AA: 126, emphasis added).

Indeed, Jung is deeply and unambiguously committed to Kantian epistemology, according to which psychic life (i.e. the Kantian 'phenomena') is all we can really know, everything else (i.e. the Kantian 'noumena') being unknowable. He expresses this commitment in passages such as:

[The psyche] will never get beyond itself. All comprehension and all that is comprehended is in itself psychic, and to that extent we are hopelessly cooped up in an exclusively psychic world. (MDR: 385)

And:

psychic happenings constitute our only, immediate experience. ... My sense impressions—for all that they force upon me a world of impenetrable objects occupying space— are psychic images, and these alone are my immediate experience ... All our knowledge is conditioned by the psyche which, because it alone is immediate, is *superlatively real*. (MMSS: 194, emphasis added)

Often, however, Jung seems to cross the boundary that separates epistemology from metaphysics and assert that the psyche is *metaphysically* primary:

I am not alluding to the vulgar notion that anything "psychic" is either nothing at all [as in eliminative materialism[11]] or at best even more tenuous than a gas [i.e. a reducible epiphenomenon, as in mainstream materialism]. *Quite the contrary;* I am of the opinion that the psyche is ... *indisputably real*. (ACU: 116, emphasis added)

Jung often uses the adjective 'real' where today's philosophers would use the term 'irreducible.' What he means by insisting that the psyche is "indisputably" or "superlatively" real is that it isn't reducible to—i.e. explainable in terms of—something non-psychic. Instead, the psyche is 'real' in the sense that it is a *fundamental* aspect of nature. This becomes clearer, for instance, in a passage of Jung's correspondence with Fr. White:

reduce something to a whim or an imagination, then it vanishes into μὴ ὄν, i.e. nothingness. I firmly believe however that the psyche is an οὐσία. (JWL: 141)

'Οὐσία' ('Oussia') is the Ancient Greek word for 'substance,' 'essence,' 'gist,' even 'being,' something that exists *in and by itself,* independently of anything else. So by claiming that the psyche is itself an οὐσία, Jung is saying that it is its own metaphysical ground or category—i.e. the 'psychic.' And as if to eliminate any possible doubt in this regard, he declares:

> The psyche deserves to be taken as a phenomenon *in its own right;* there are no grounds at all for regarding it as a mere epiphenomenon (ONP: 8-9, emphasis added)

Jung goes even further and argues that the psyche is a necessary condition for the *very existence of everything else,* not only our knowledge thereof. For instance, he states that "Existence is only real when it is conscious to somebody" (AJ: 11) and that "Psyche is existent, *it is even existence itself'* (PR: 12, emphasis added). At one point he elaborates on this fundamental metaphysical claim:

> The psyche is the world's pivot: not only is it *the one great condition for the existence of a world at all,* it is also an intervention in the existing natural order, and *no one can say with certainty where this intervention will finally end.* (ONP: 151, emphasis added)

So perhaps it never ends, in which case the world *is* psychic. In a letter to Pauli, Jung even dares to define physics as "a science *of ideas* with a material label," which he then rushes to point out—lest he inadvertently confesses to his covert philosophical inclinations—is an "epistemological definition, not a practical one" (AA: 111, emphasis added). One can almost feel the tension between what Jung senses intuitively and what he allows himself to state overtly, so to manage how Pauli and others perceive his work.

Nonetheless, the extrapolation of epistemic points into metaphysics territory is not necessarily wrong or even inappropriate. After all, all we have to make inferences about the nature of reality is our *knowledge of* reality. The fundamental limitations of knowledge can, and should, play a decisive role in our metaphysical views. Where the reach of knowledge decreases, our sense of implausibility should increase (cf. Kastrup 2018). This is precisely how Jung seems to think.

For all these reasons, I submit that, once he is faced with the need to postulate something beyond the *human* psyche to account for what Pauli calls the "structural elements of cosmic order," Jung cannot help but to implicitly *extrapolate the metaphysical essence of the psyche itself* past the psyche's ostensibly human boundaries. Jung thinks of the transpersonal ground beyond ourselves as an extension of the psychic "substance" —οὐσία— which not only links living beings together, but also living beings and the inorganic world.

Now, recall that, as discussed earlier, the essential nature of the psyche is *experiential*. Consequently, insofar as they share the same metaphysical ground as the psyche, *matter and spirit*—as opposite extremes in the psychic spectrum— *must also be experiential*. Jung's theories thus imply a form of metaphysical idealism:[12] all existence unfolds in a "greater and more comprehensive consciousness," in the form of a play of experiences.

Idealism is a monist position—i.e. it states that there is but *one* intrinsic essence underlying all existence—distinct from dualism. Therefore, the dualist interpretation of synchronicity discussed earlier isn't consistent with the broader context of Jung's thought. It is not a problem to discard it, though, for we no longer need dualism anyway: the so-called physical world, under idealism, is already essentially psychic *in and of itself*. As such, it can directly express meaning without a metaphysically distinct 'world-soul' manipulating it from behind the scenes. In a sense, the physical world already *is* the 'world-soul.' The qualities we attribute to physicality—form, color, temperature, consistency, concreteness, etc.—are merely appearances; they are how a fundamentally psychic 'world-soul' *presents* itself on the screen of our perceptions. Such idealist interpretation allows all of Jung's key metaphysics-related contentions—not only synchronicity—to cohere elegantly and parsimoniously. I shall discuss this in more depth later.

For now, however, we must address some passages in Jung's writings that, at first sight and out of context, may seem to contradict the idealist interpretation proposed above. For instance:

> Although there is no form of existence that is not mediated to us psychically and only psychically, it would hardly do to say that everything is merely psychic. (ONP: 149)

To properly interpret passages such as this, we must keep in mind that by 'psychic' Jung often means *properly* psychic—i.e. conscious. So he is simply acknowledging that not everything is a *conscious* experience, for there are also *un*conscious experiences—i.e. phenomenal states not accessible to the ego through introspection.

Indeed, when Jung is being more guarded and careful, trying *not* to antagonize the predominantly materialist views of his time, he seems to deliberately exploit the ambiguity of the word 'psychic.' Here is another example: in a letter written in March 1953, Pauli admonishes Jung to *"not once again* make too much of the *psychic factor"* (AA: 106, original emphasis). To which Jung replies, in a reconciliatory and accommodating tone:

> We can say of an object that it is psychic when it is ascertainable only as a concept. But if it has features that indicate its non-psychic *autonomous* existence, we naturally tend to accept it as non-psychic. (AA: 113, emphasis added)

By associating the "non-psychic" with something

"autonomous" — i.e. outside deliberate volitional control — Jung is using the qualifier 'psychic' in the more restrictive sense of *properly* psychic. So the statement does not contradict idealism, in that it only acknowledges that there is something beyond *consciousness*, not necessarily beyond experience. Yet, the wording is just ambiguous enough that it could be interpreted by Pauli as an acknowledgment of the possibility of a material world outside and independent of experience.

An even more important interpretative avenue is this: when he says that the psychoid archetypes are "part of the substance of the psychic," Jung clearly means that the *categorical basis* — i.e. the *metaphysical essence* — of the archetypes is psychic, *experiential*, even though they manifest themselves beyond the *human* psyche. However, when he doubts that the archetypes are exclusively psychic (cf. e.g. ONP: 166), he means that the *human* psyche isn't the sole locus of archetypal manifestation, the latter taking place in the physical world at large as well. Although apparently contradictory, these statements are perfectly reconcilable if interpreted charitably. In one case, 'psychic' refers to the metaphysical essence, whereas in the other case it refers to *human* experiential boundaries.

Here is an analogy to help clarify the point: imagine farmers who live in the Egyptian inland desert and the only instance of water they've ever seen is the river Nile; they've never seen rain, snow, lakes, ice or the sea. Imagine further that they call the substance or essence of the river 'riverness,' instead of water, for they've never experienced water in any other form or manifestation. In regard to the psychic, we are in an analogous position to that of the farmers: the only instance of psychic contents we ever become directly acquainted with is our own human psyche, so we refer to the metaphysical essence of these contents as, well, *psychic*; just as the farmers refer to the essence of the river as 'riverness.' However, analogously to how water manifests itself *beyond* the river Nile — in the form of oceans, lakes, hail, etc.—the psychic essence also manifests itself *beyond* the human psyche, even though we cannot ascertain it directly. This is what Jung means when he denies that the archetypes are exclusively psychic: they are not restricted to the *human* psyche. Nonetheless, the archetypes are still psychic *in essence*, in the same way that the oceans and rain are still 'riverness'—i.e. water—in essence, even though they are not encompassed by the river Nile. This latter point is what Jung means when he claims that the psychoid archetypes "are part of the substance of the psychic."

There is a more conspicuous passage in which Jung seems to contradict idealism by appearing to favor a different metaphysics:

> Since psyche and matter are contained in one and the same world, and moreover are in continuous contact with one another and ultimately rest on irrepresentable, transcendental factors, it is not only possible but fairly probable, even, that psyche and matter are two different aspects of one and the same thing. (ONP: 148)

One might hastily conclude from reading this passage out of context that Jung's favored metaphysics is dual-aspect monism: the notion that psyche and matter are merely two different aspects of a concealed, fundamental metaphysical substrate that, in turn, is *neither* psychic *nor* material in essence (cf. Stubenberg 2018: Section 8.3). This, of course, would contradict Jung's stated position that the psychic is its own οὐσία—substance, essence, being—for in the case of dual-aspect monism the psychic would be merely a view or representation of a *non-psychic* substance. So what is going on?

Careful analysis reveals a very different point here than an appeal to dual-aspect monism. Allow me to elaborate.

First, let us clarify what Jung means by claiming that matter rests on "transcendental factors": as recognized by Kant already in the 18th century, all we can become directly acquainted with are explicit *perceptions*—i.e. conscious contents of the psyche that merely *represent* an external world. The non-experiential, non-psychic, essentially material substrate that—according to mainstream materialism—supposedly causes these perceptions by stimulating our sense organs cannot be known as it is in itself. As such, insofar as it *can* be known for sure, matter is merely an inference, a theoretical abstraction *of* ego-consciousness (cf. e.g. Kastrup 2018). In Jung's words:

> the only form of existence we know of immediately is psychic. We might as well say ... that *physical existence is merely an inference,* since we know of matter only in so far as we perceive psychic images transmitted by the senses. (PR: 11, emphasis added)

Jung then states that the psyche, like matter, also rests on "transcendental factors." But since the experiential contents of ego-consciousness are precisely the only thing we *can* become directly acquainted with, what does he mean by that statement? Here again, the crux of the matter is Jung's inconsistent usage of the term 'psyche' to refer sometimes to the psyche *proper*, other times to the *foundation* of the psyche—i.e. the collective unconscious—and yet other times to the psyche *as a whole*. The claim that the "psyche [rests on] transcendental factors" gives us the clue we need to figure out which denotation is meant in this particular context.

Indeed, in the discussion that immediately precedes the passage wherein Jung *seems* to suggest dual-aspect monism, he focuses entirely on highlighting the unknowability of the *psychoid* realm of the psyche—i.e. the archetypes in the collective unconscious. Therefore, by claiming that the psyche rests on "transcendental factors," he is alluding to the *collective unconscious*, a part of the psyche that transcends our ability to become directly acquainted with. The psyche *proper*—i.e. ego-consciousness—is, by definition, *not* transcendental; indeed, it's the one thing we have direct access to! So the psyche proper doesn't belong in the comparison with matter that Jung attempts to make—at any rate, not on the basis of the argument he puts forward to justify the comparison.

It is the collective unconscious alone that Jung means to equate with matter, not the psyche as a whole. Both the collective unconscious and matter, as they are in themselves, cannot be apprehended directly but just inferred from their effects on ego-consciousness. This is much clearer and unambiguous, for instance, in Jung's correspondence with Pauli, in which the two men discuss the equivalence between the *"mundus archetypus"* (i.e. the collective unconscious, the domain of the archetypes) and the *"physis"* (i.e. the physical world):

> The wholeness of man [which includes ego-consciousness] holds the *middle position*, namely between the *mundus archetypus*, which is real, because it acts, and the *physis*, which is just as real, because it acts. The principle of both, however, is unknown and therefore not ascertainable. Moreover, there are grounds for supposing that *both are different aspects of one and the same principle* (AA: 101, emphasis added).

That is, the *physis* may in some sense be equivalent to the *mundus archetypus*, but not to the psyche as a whole. Unlike the 'principles' of the *physis* and the *mundus archetypus*, that of the psyche *proper*—i.e. ego-consciousness—*is* ascertainable. As such, the psyche proper is part of the "middle position," not of the world of matter.

One doesn't even need to appeal to Jung's technical writings to see that what he equates with matter is the *collective unconscious*, not the psyche as a whole. In a letter, he states it in very plain and unambiguous language, almost as if he were trying to dispel any remaining doubt about the very point in contention here:

> So far as we can see, the collective unconscious is identical with Nature to the extent that Nature herself, including matter, is unknown to us. I have nothing against the assumption that the psyche is a quality of matter or matter the concrete aspect of the psyche, *provided that "psyche" is defined as the collective unconscious.* (L, Vol. 2: 540)

Such inconsistent usage of the term 'psyche' occurs frequently in Jung's corpus. For instance, within the space of three paragraphs in a letter to Pauli, Jung claims first that "the *psyche is not a metaphysical concept* but an empirical one" (AA: 112, emphasis added), just to state, two paragraphs later, that "matter, *psyche,* and spirit are in themselves of an unknown nature and thus *are metaphysical* or postulated" (AA: 113, emphasis added). In the first statement, what Jung means by 'psyche' is the psyche *proper,* whose contents we can inspect directly through introspection. In the second sentence, he means by it the collective unconscious, which we cannot inspect directly but only infer on the basis of its *effects* on ego-consciousness.

Therefore, I submit that the correct interpretation of Jung's seemingly dual-aspect monist hypothesis above is the following: both the *objective psyche* (more specifically, the collective unconscious) and the *objective world* (i.e. matter) are *conceptual inferences* of ego-consciousness, neither being amenable to direct inspection. All we can know about them is their *effects* on ego-consciousness, caused by their *impinging* on it, either through the sense organs (in the case of the objective world) or through a shared, internal psychic boundary (in the case of the objective psyche). Therefore, it is conceivable—even likely, because of parsimony considerations—that the objective world and the objective psyche are essentially the same entity, impinging on our subjectivity in two different ways.

Once one understands what Jung is actually trying to say here, the symmetry and elegance of his vision become clear. The external world we perceive with our sense organs, *as it is in itself,* is transcendent, autonomous, independent of our volition, seemingly separate from us, animated by its own impetus and organized according to archetypes (cf. synchronicity). We perceive this world because its dynamisms impinge on ego-consciousness through the sense organs, generating the autonomous imagery of perception. In an entirely analogous manner, the collective unconscious, *as it is in itself,* is also transcendent, autonomous, independent of our volition, seemingly separate from us, animated by its own impetus and organized according to archetypes. We perceive the collective unconscious because its dynamisms impinge on ego-consciousness through a shared, internal psychic boundary, generating the autonomous imagery of dreams and visions. Do you see the elegant symmetry of this view?

For Jung, *the external physical world and the collective unconscious are one and the same thing presenting itself to us in two different ways.* Both impinge on ego-consciousness, generating autonomous imagery we can witness but not control. Put simply, the supposedly material substrate underlying perception isn't material at all; *it is the collective unconscious itself.* In a 1954 letter to Fr. White, Jung brings this notion to life:

> the collective unconscious [is] the sphere, where the paint is made that colours the world, where the light is created, that makes shine the splendor of the dawn, the lines and shapes of all form, the sound that fills the orbit, the thought that illuminates the darkness of the void. (JWL: 241)

All this is illustrated in Figure 4. The collective unconscious is both an internal segment of the human psyche and the external environment that surrounds the human psyche. It impinges on ego-consciousness both from within (thereby generating the objective imagery of dreams and visions) and without (thereby generating the equally objective imagery on the screen of perception, through the mediation of the sense organs). The result of the latter impingement is what we call the 'physical world.' As such, the collective unconscious is responsible for *all* seemingly autonomous imagery we consciously experience. We, human beings, by virtue of surrounding the *"mundus archetypus"* and being surrounded by the *"physis,"* occupy the "middle position" between the two.

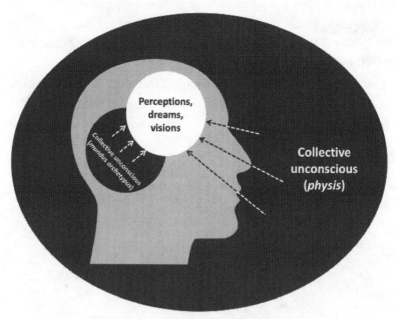

Figure 4. We both surround and are surrounded by the collective unconscious, the objective part of the psyche that impinges on ego-consciousness and creates the autonomous imagery of perceptions, dreams and visions.

Now, as we've seen earlier, both consciousness and the unconscious are essentially *experiential*. So by positing that the collective unconscious and the physical world are the same thing manifest in two ways, Jung is again implying that the physical world is also essentially experiential. The resulting metaphysics is not dual-aspect monism but, once again, idealism. More specifically, it is what today's analytic philosophers call 'objective idealism' (Chalmers 2018).

According to objective idealism, there is a world out there, outside the volitional control of ego-consciousness, but it is a world constituted by *transpersonal experiences*. These transpersonal experiences—objective from the perspective of the ego—impinge on ego-consciousness in two ways, creating *autonomous imagery in both cases*. Hence, according to Jung's hardly disguised metaphysical views, all existence can be reduced to—i.e. explained in terms of—phenomenality.

In the discussion above, I've argued that, for Jung, we can become directly acquainted only with the psychic, everything else being merely inferred. There are passages, however, in which Jung may seem to contradict this. For instance:

> To inquire into the *substance* of what has been observed is possible in natural science only where there is an Archimedean point outside. For the psyche, no such outside standpoint exists—only the psyche can observe the psyche. Consequently, knowledge of the psychic substance is impossible for us. (ACU: 207, original emphasis)[13]

By "Archimedean point" Jung means an external vantage point from which the defining characteristics of the substance in question can be consciously observed and *contrasted* with something else that *isn't* the substance. For instance, mass is defined in terms of having inertia, which massless particles— such as photons—do not have. Whereas we consciously observe that mass resists changes in speed and direction of movement, we observe no such resistance when it comes to light. That we can consciously observe the *contrasting* behavior of mass and light from an external, Archimedean vantage point is what allows us to conceptually define them both, in terms of each other. But when it comes to the psyche, there is no such external vantage point.

Notice, however, that all this means is that we cannot *conceptually define* the psychic as we conceptually define e.g. mass (namely, as that which has inertia, in contrast to pure energy) and energy (namely, as that which performs work, in contrast to pure mass). After all, we cannot take an external vantage point so as to contrast the psychic with something *non*-psychic; "we are hopelessly cooped up in an exclusively psychic world." One could try to define the psychic as 'that which is inherently experiential,' but such definition is circular: 'experiential' is just another word for 'psychic.' This is the difficulty Jung is alluding to in the passage quoted above.

Be that as it may, the impossibility of conceptually defining the psychic—as desirable in the natural sciences—does not mean that we can't *become acquainted* with it and therefore know it in this latter sense. Babies become acquainted with their entire experiential environment before conceptual thinking even begins to develop in them. Indeed, it is impossible to *not* become acquainted with the psychic, for it is all we ever have; it is the water wherein we are always swimming. For Jung, we cannot 'know' the psychic merely in the sense that we say fish cannot know water.

Consequently, when Jung claims "knowledge of the psychic substance is impossible for us," he means merely that we can't *conceptually define* it as a metaphysical ground, for we are immersed in it like fish in water. But we certainly know the psychic in the sense of being acquainted with it, with or without scientific definitions to accompany such acquaintance. As a matter of fact, the psychic is the *only* metaphysical ground we can ever be directly acquainted with, for "All comprehension and all that is comprehended is in itself psychic." Therefore, the passage quoted above in no way contradicts my earlier argumentation.

Today, philosophers can persuasively argue for metaphysical idealism in a manner that is entirely consistent with modern science (cf. e.g. Kastrup 2014, 2016a). In fact, metaphysical idealism is arguably the only option left for making sense of the latest experimental results in fields such as quantum mechanics (cf. e.g. Kastrup 2019). Perhaps if Jung had been exposed to a complete and coherent formulation of idealism that answered all the key criticisms commonly leveraged against it, he would have allowed himself to express his metaphysical views more openly.

Nonetheless, despite myriad seeming contradictions if one interprets his words uncharitably and out of context, there is an interpretation of Jung's metaphysics-related contentions that reconciles them all: the metaphysical essence of *everything*— spirit, psyche and the physical universe at large—is the same essence we become directly acquainted with through human experience—i.e. a *phenomenal* essence.

Chapter 6

Religion

[The modern attitude towards the divine can be summarized in the words,] "Let's make sure the divine takes good care of us. But as for finding what, in reality, the divine might possibly need: let it look after itself." From here onwards one can sit back and watch how the idea of looking after the gods starts, almost by magic, vanishing from the western world. … And now it never for a moment occurs to us that the divine might be suffering, aching from our neglect; that the sacred desperately longs for our attention far more than we in some occasional, unconscious spasm might feel a brief burst of embarrassed longing for it.
Peter Kingsley, in *Catafalque* (2018)

The notion that the substrate of all reality—both inner and outer worlds—is essentially experiential has obvious religious overtones, in that such substrate could also be described as an omniscient, omnipresent, omnipotent, supraordinate universal mind, of which we are all dissociated centers of awareness. Jung has come to this view by extrapolating the "substance" of his own conscious psyche both outward, to the world at large, and inward, to the transpersonal, unconscious foundation of his psyche.

As we've seen, it is Kantian epistemology that intellectually motivates Jung to take "psychic substance" as nature's sole fundamental ground. Yet he clearly also had an innate experiential disposition to extend the psychic sphere beyond personal human boundaries anyway, which can be seen, for instance, in a famous passage of his autobiography:

At times I feel as if I am spread out over the landscape and inside things, and am myself living in every tree, in the splashing of the waves, in the clouds and the animals that come and go, in the procession of the seasons. (MDR: 252)

Echoing this, in a metaphysically pregnant passage of his technical writings, Jung describes the collective unconscious as

a boundless expanse ... where I experience the other in myself and the other-than-myself experiences me. [It] is sheer objectivity, as wide as the world and open to all the world. ... There *I am utterly one with the world,* so much a part of it that I forget all too easily who I really am. "Lost in oneself" is a good way of describing this state. *But this self is the world,* if only a consciousness could see it. (ACU: 22, emphasis added)

Here we have Jung not only claiming unambiguously that we are one with the world itself, but also that this identity can be recognized *experientially.* The implication, once again, is that we and the world at large are all parts of some boundless universal mind, in the most comprehensive sense of the world.

Some authors suggest that the collective unconscious consists merely of a common genetic inheritance (cf. e.g. Stevens 2001: 51-52). If each person inherits their own private copy of the collective unconscious from their parents, there is no need to postulate a transpersonal metaphysical ground psychically linking people together; the collective unconscious is collective merely by virtue of the fact that everyone has a copy of it—or so the story goes.

However, not only do Jung's own words—as just quoted above—contradict this unambiguously, when it comes to the extended notion of synchronicity discussed between Jung and Pauli a transpersonal psychic ground cannot be avoided. After all, the physical world at large receives no genetic inheritance from human beings! If the archetypes organize the physical world just as they do human psychic activity, then there has to be some common, unitary, underlying metaphysical *field* that links everyone and everything together. Jung proceeds to identify this unifying field with God itself: "Nature, the psyche, and life appear to me like divinity unfolded" (MDR: 306). I shall elaborate more on this shortly. For now, though, bear with me.

The one technical book wherein Jung seems to give himself permission to discuss religious metaphysics more directly—and therefore say more about divinity and its relation to us and the physical world—is *Answer to Job* (AJ). Consider, for instance, the following passage:

> Psychologism represents a still primitive mode of thinking, with the help of which one hopes to conjure the reality of the soul out of existence. ... *One would be very ill advised to identify me with such a childish standpoint.* However, I have been asked so often whether I believe in God or not that I am somewhat concerned lest I be taken for an adherent of "psychologism" far more commonly than I suspect. What most people overlook or seem to be unable to understand is the fact that I regard the psyche as *real*. They believe only in physical facts, and must consequently come to the conclusion that either the uranium itself or the laboratory equipment created the atom bomb. That is no less absurd than the assumption that a non-real psyche is responsible for it. *God is an obvious psychic and non-physical fact,* i.e., a fact that can be established psychically but not physically. (AJ: 133, emphasis added)

To assert the "obvious psychic and non-physical fact" of God's existence is a bold step for the metaphysically reticent Jung. The assertion is particularly significant because it happens in a passage wherein Jung also distances himself from psychologism: given the context, it is impossible to argue that Jung is merely psychologizing the notion of God. For him God is *real* in the same sense that the psyche, too, is real — i.e. irreducible. Under Jung's metaphysics, to place God in the psychic sphere does *not* in any way diminish God's reality or significance, for everything that truly is can only be psychic. This is what "most people overlook or seem to be unable to understand."

Despite being often misunderstood, Jung is very consistent in this position. Already in an earlier work, he had been even more explicit in distancing himself from, as well as denouncing, the mistake of psychologizing God. After stating that materialism was the first inevitable error of our de-spiritualized culture, he goes on to say:

> The second inevitable *mistake* is *psychologism*: if god is anything, he must be an illusion derived from certain motives, from fear, for instance, from will to power, or from repressed sexuality. (PR: 103, emphasis added)

In general, whenever he attempts to explain things in psychological terms, Jung shouldn't be interpreted as denying the reality or significance of what he is explaining (cf. PA: 8-9) — i.e. he shouldn't be taken for "an adherent of psychologism." Instead, the psychological terms are simply the natural and appropriate language for making sense of the *irreducibly experiential* reality he is attempting to elucidate. For Jung, making sense of life and world in psychological terms merely acknowledges their fundamentally psychic nature.

But can we regard *Answer to Job* as a true religious confession by Jung? Could it, instead, be simply a detached psychological analysis of scripture written — for maximum effect — in metaphorical language?

Admittedly, the book is written in a way that leaves room for different interpretations almost until the end. For most of the text, it remains unclear whether Jung is analyzing the writers of scripture, carrying out an exercise in scriptural exegesis, or discussing his own personal religious views. On face value, the latter possibility is the one that best matches the tone and style of the text, but it's difficult to be certain.

However, in the closing of the book, after reassuringly clarifying that "the account I have given ... corresponds to a process of differentiation in human consciousness" (AJ: 141), Jung immediately adds these extraordinary words:

> since ... the archetypes in question are not mere objects of the [personal human] mind, but are also autonomous factors, i.e., *living subjects,* the differentiation of consciousness can be understood as the effect of the intervention of *transcendentally conditioned dynamisms.* (AJ: 141, emphasis added)

What a wonderfully technical way to embrace religious metaphysics! Instead of "autonomous living subjects" who "intervene" in human (inner) life through "transcendentally conditioned dynamisms," we might as well talk of angels, demons and the whole celestial entourage guiding and messing with human psychic evolution. As a matter of fact, Jung himself states that the daemons, "relatively autonomous (fragmentary) personalities, ... correspond to angels and demons" (JWL: 70).

No, I am not mocking Jung and would never dare to do so; I know better by now. I am simply marveling at his ability to be so candid and clear about his religious views while—rather miraculously—*preserving plausible deniability* that he is straying away from scientific psychology at all.

At the risk of repeating myself, I must emphasize again that, while some interpret *Answer to Job* as mere psychologizing of religion—i.e. as relegating religious ideas to the position of subjective epiphenomena, as opposed to objective spiritual realities—under Jung's metaphysical idealism *to be psychic is to be ultimately real;* for there is nothing but the psychic. In a 1947 letter to Pastor Werner Niederer, Jung explains:

> Above all it must be understood that there is *objective psychic existence,* and that psychological explanation is not necessarily psychologizing, i.e., subjectivizing. (JWL: 293, original emphasis)

So by placing angels, demons and God itself in the sphere of the psychic, Jung is far from denying their reality; much to the contrary: he is precisely attributing to these entities the same felt reality you and I, as psychic agents, have. *You and I, too, are just relatively sophisticated daemons immersed in the ocean of the collective unconscious.* Even the physical world itself, as we've seen in the previous chapter, is a manifestation of the collective unconscious. There is nothing that *isn't* psychic.

And to those guilty of the "prejudice that the deity is outside man" (PR: 72)—who feel that placing God and its entourage in the psychic sphere somehow *confines* them—Jung has these enlightening words to say:

> The psyche reaches so far beyond the boundary line of consciousness that the latter could be easily compared to an island in the ocean. While the island is small and narrow, the ocean is immensely wide and deep, so that *if it is a question of space, it does not matter whether the gods are inside or outside.* (PR: 102, emphasis added)

This is Jung's genius. Whereas the mainstream might read a form of neutering of religion into his contention that the gods are psychic—and then ironically nod in deluded agreement— those who actually understand him know that, for Jung, religion is as significant as anything can possibly be. His brilliance is in framing his message so that it mirrors the foolish expectations of the mainstream—and therefore masquerades *as* mainstream—while conveying its intended meaning fully, openly, without any concession or compromise, to those with the eyes to see it. Jung hides his religious views in plain sight.

Consider, for instance, Don Cupitt's words in his famous 1984 TV series, *Sea of Faith*:

> [Jung] always accepted that natural science gives us our only knowledge of the external physical world. But there is *another* world ... the inner world of the psyche. ... for Jung, religion is about that inner world ... all religious truths and religious objects *are simply psychological*. (Emphasis added)

Here we see how effectively Jung's ideas masquerade as mainstream and hide in plain sight. The condescending confining of religion to the "simply psychological"—which is presented as a world *other* than the physical—is bound to sound reassuring to the vulgar materialist spirit of this time.

Yes, for Jung religion is indeed about the psychic; but so is everything else. For him even the external world beyond the *personal* psyche—which we perceive via the five senses—is in itself essentially psychic and organized by archetypes. We are, and are immersed in, the psychic. A physical world outside and independent of the psychic sphere is only a theoretical abstraction, known only conceptually and ultimately unreal. It is precisely for being "simply psychological" that "religious truths and religious objects" are *real* in the same way that the world perceived through the senses is real. The world of the psyche is not separate from the external world; instead, it *includes* the latter. But what fraction of the TV audience that hears Cupitt's affable words realizes this?

The possibility that Jung uses *Answer to Job* to make a hardly camouflaged religious confession becomes even more compelling when we consider that—according to Catrine Clay (2016: 339-340)—the completion of the book gave him the happiest moment of his life and made him feel that he had redeemed his father, a protestant pastor. A book whose completion gives its author the happiest moment of his life cannot be a detached analytical exercise; instead, it must speak to the deepest, most intimate aspects of his inner life.

That such is the case with *Answer to Job* was clear to those close to Jung. For instance, Fr. White "had never supposed that [Jung] would publish *so personal a document*" (JWL: 289 emphasis added). Jung himself admits that writing *Answer to Job* was "an experience charged with emotion" (MDR: 243). Peter Kingsley's ridiculously well documented account vividly illustrates this:

> *Answer to Job* swept through him [i.e. Jung], along with his home and household, like a storm. ... For the months that he was writing, then revising, the text there were times when he not only hardly slept but hardly shaved; hardly washed. ... He shut himself away for hours and worked until he was exhausted. Then he became moody and often furious, lashed out for no reason, was crude and rude. (Kingsley 2018: 354)

These are hardly the reactions of someone engaged in the writing of a detached analysis of scripture. No, clearly *Answer to Job* was personal, very personal. And it is in this context that a couple of the book's most significant messages, as summarized in two key passages quoted below, are so revealing of Jung's religious thought. Here is the first:

> It was only very lately that we realized (or rather, are beginning to realize) that *God is Reality itself and therefore*—last but not least—*man*. (AJ: 48, emphasis added)

That is, God *is* the unifying experiential field at the ground of all reality, including ourselves. As dissociated psychic complexes or daemons of this field—"bits of God that had become independent" (MDR: 86)—our essence *is* the field. And so, in an important sense, God is us.

In an earlier work, Jung had already given indications that he tended towards this notion. There, he asserts that "there is psychological justification" for the view, held by our forefathers, which posited

the individual soul [i.e. personal psyche] to be dependent upon a world-system of the spirit. [Our forefathers] assumed without question that this system was a being with a will and consciousness ... and they called this being God, *the quintessence of reality.* (MMSS: 192, emphasis added)

In asserting that "there is psychological justification" for this view, Jung equates the "world-system of the spirit" with his own concept of the collective unconscious (cf. MMSS: 191-192). Therefore, here Jung is already confessing to sympathizing with the equation 'collective unconscious = God,' a position—as we shall discuss now—that congealed later in his life.

Indeed, here is the second key passage of *Answer to Job*:

The unconscious wants to flow into consciousness in order to reach the light, but at the same time it continually thwarts itself, because it would rather remain unconscious. *That is to say, God wants to become man, but not quite.* (AJ: 123, emphasis added)

For Jung, *God itself,* as an irreducible metaphysical reality, is to be found in the collective unconscious; or rather, it is *indistinguishable* from the unconscious:

It is only through the psyche that we can establish that God acts upon us, but we are unable to distinguish whether these actions emanate from God or from the unconscious. We cannot tell whether God and the unconscious are two different entities. (AJ: 139)

What is meant by this is *more* than to say that the God-*image* is derived from the collective unconscious—corresponding to the archetype of the self—which is empirically verifiable and standard Jungian doctrine. Here, instead, Jung is speculating about a *metaphysical identity* between God and the collective unconscious.[14] The implication, if he is correct, is that the very *categorical basis*—the *metaphysical essence*—of the unconscious is the same as that of the divinity; and, as we've seen, this essence is *experiential*. As such, Jung's God is an all-encompassing overmind, of which we are diminutive segments, daemons, dissociated psychic complexes.

Consequently, given the extended version of synchronicity that places the collective unconscious at the metaphysical foundation of the physical world itself, the whole of nature— organic and inorganic—is "divinity unfolded." Jung's views in this regard echo Spinoza's, for whom the essence of all nature was God. The difference is that, whereas Spinoza reserved for God its own mysterious categorical basis, for Jung the essence of nature *and* God is *known*: it is "the 'substance' of all phenomena of the inner world" (AA: 125). By epistemically resisting the attribution of reality to anything non-psychic—and thereby relegating non-psychic matter and spirit to the status of mere *concepts* (cf. AA: 112-113)—Jung ends up finding God in a metaphysically extended form of psyche, far transcending human boundaries. The divinity, for him, is a unifying, universal, all-encompassing field of phenomenality.

And now we're finally about to reach the climax of this little book: an elucidation of what, in my view, is the most important point Jung has ever made, the crown jewel of his immense legacy. Indeed, if I were to pick *one* message for humanity to heed from across Jung's entire corpus—one with the potential to transform our lives—it would be what is discussed below. So, without further ado, let's get to it.

As Jung himself put it,

Meaninglessness inhibits fullness of life and is therefore equivalent to illness. Meaning makes a great many things endurable—perhaps everything. (MDR: 373)

So what is the meaning of our lives as tiny little daemons within the unfathomable immensity of the collective unconscious? What is the purpose of our powerless existence before the overwhelming might of God? To put it more simply, *why does God need us,* puny creatures struggling to survive on this planet, in a corner of an unremarkable galaxy, assailed by all sorts of superior powers both from within (the demons in the collective unconscious, which inflict unbearable anxieties and disillusionment upon us) and without (the destructive forces of nature, which threaten our bodily integrity)? Framed in this manner, it is extraordinarily difficult to find a persuasive and satisfying answer to these questions. But if we can't find one, our lives may be all for nothing; our pain and suffering may serve no purpose; our joy and elation may be ephemeral phantasms with no significance.

This question of meaning has been at the forefront of human life since at least the Enlightenment, in the 18th-century. Whereas religions would have provided some measure of reassurance before the Enlightenment, modern humans find themselves at the mercy of a shallow and reductive worldview—the spirit of this time—prone to driving us to existential despair. And here is where Jung has come to play an indispensable role in our history: that of re-opening a compelling and satisfying horizon of meaning for modern humanity. He summarizes his contention in a seemingly innocent little passage of—what else?—*Answer to Job*:

> what does man possess that God does not have? Because of his littleness, puniness, and defencelessness against the Almighty, he possesses ... *a somewhat keener consciousness based on self-reflection*: he must, in order to survive, always be mindful of his impotence. God has no need of this circumspection, for nowhere does he come up against an insuperable obstacle that would force him to hesitate and hence make him *reflect on himself*. (AJ: 14-15, emphasis added)

Self-reflection—i.e. conscious meta-cognition, meta-consciousness, our ability to know *that* we experience, to separate ourselves, as subjects, from our own objectified psychic contents—is what God needs us for! Although he has superior and even omniscient knowledge, God cannot "*consult* his total knowledge" (AJ: 37, emphasis added)—i.e. the divinity cannot *deliberately introspect* as we can. Instead, God is both instinctual and spiritual, surrounding us from both ends of the psychic spectrum (see Figure 1 again), but not *conscious* as Jung defines the word. Only *through us* does the divinity attain consciousness. "As the eye to the sun, so the [human] soul corresponds to God," explains Jung in wonderfully aphoristic words (PA: 10); "an eye destined to behold the light" (PA: 13).

It is because of this that "God wants to become man" by means of the biblical Incarnation. *We are incarnate sparks of divine being,* here to render a service to God. As such, "man's life should be sacrificial, that is, offered up to an idea greater than man" (PR: 94). This greater idea is divine self-awareness.

While *Answer to Job* is indeed an account of a "process of differentiation in human consciousness," it is equally an account of the inception and growth of God's own self-awareness, enabled by our service. Jung continues elsewhere:

> That is the meaning of divine service, or the service which man
> can render to God, that light may emerge from the darkness,
> that the Creator may become conscious of His creation, and
> man conscious of himself. (MDR: 371)

We can render this service to God because, "just as the unconscious
affects us, so the increase in our consciousness affects the
unconscious" (MDR: 358). This way, simply by reflecting upon
life and world we already automatically contribute to God's self-
awareness, whether we know it or not. Jung's view implies that
human life has *inevitable* meaning.

Moreover, not only is human self-reflection the meaning
of our existence, in a sense it is also what brings meaning and
existence into being to begin with: Jung speaks of "existence
becoming real through *reflection* in consciousness," for "Without
the *reflecting* consciousness of man the world is a gigantic
meaningless machine" (JWL: 236 including note 51, emphasis
added).

So here you have it: in very few words, Jung offers a plausible
and satisfying answer to what I consider to be life's most critical
question, filling the vacuum left open by the 'death of God' in the
19th-century (cf. Taylor 2007) and restoring our sense of purpose
and meaning. If only his message were more widespread and
better understood.

But in Jung's own view, the truly decisive question is somewhat
different (cf. MDR: 357): Are we, as finite human beings,
related to something infinite or not? As argued throughout this
book, his writings imply that the answer is yes: the collective
unconscious is the matrix of all existence—both inner and
outer—and, therefore, effectively infinite and eternal. We, as
relatively sophisticated daemons—but *daemons* nonetheless—of

the collective unconscious, are thus surely related to something infinite.

Yet, throughout his technical corpus, Jung stops short of overtly admitting this so as to preserve a semblance of metaphysical neutrality. Only in the final years of his life, as he became increasingly engrossed in his autobiography, did he allow himself more latitude to confess his thoughts on the question.

Indeed, already in the prologue of his autobiography, Jung offers a striking analogy: he compares life to the visible part of a plant, which rises in spring and decays in the fall. But the rhizome or root system, lying hidden in the soil, endures from year to year. What seems to be an ephemeral phenomenon when contemplated from above ground proves to be just a manifestation of an enduring hidden core. For Jung, thus, our individual lives are just like visible shoots sprouting from the eternal, invisible matrix of the collective unconscious. Our deaths are no more final than the autumn decay: the core of what is truly going on— of what we truly *are*—remains unaffected, ready to sprout new life in the following spring (cf. MDR: 18).

Jung goes on to relate two dreams that gave him a profound insight into the nature of personal identity. In the first dream, he is at his house in Küsnacht when four unidentified flying objects appear in the sky. One of them looks like a projector, with a circular lens attached to the main body. Unlike the other three, this latter object stands still in the air, pointing straight at Jung. Upon awakening, he interpreted this to mean that his empirical personality—his ego-body system—was merely a projection of something transcendent and enduring (cf. MDR: 355).

In the second dream, Jung wanders into a wayside chapel. Just in front of the altar he sees a yogi, sitting on the floor in a lotus position and meditating with his eyes closed. When Jung gets closer, he realizes that the yogi has his (Jung's) face. Startled, he awakes with the following thought:

"Aha, so he is the one who is meditating me. He has a dream and I am it." I knew that when he awakened, I would no longer be. ... My self retires into meditation and meditates my earthly form. (MDR: 355-356)

Jung concludes from these two dreams that our true self either *is*, or *resides in*, the collective unconscious (cf. MDR: 356), whereas our empirical personality—i.e. the visible ego-body system—is somehow generated, projected or meditated into existence by this true self.

The question of whether our true self *is*, or merely *resides in*, the collective unconscious is a relevant one. In the latter case, the true self—the meditating yogi, the flying projector—is a kind of meta-daemon of the collective unconscious, with its own history and dispositions. Our empirical personality arises then as a dissociated complex *within* the meta-daemon. Upon bodily death, we simply 'fall back' on the meta-daemon, thus retaining some degree of differentiation and individual identity.

However, if our true self *is* the collective unconscious, then it is the same for all of us, even for all living creatures. Death means the end of individual identity and a return to an undifferentiated state, akin to what Schopenhauer described as the "one eye of the world which looks out from all knowing creatures" (Schopenhauer & Payne 1969, Vol. 1: 198).

Unfortunately, Jung does not elaborate enough on this for us to discern his thoughts in this regard with more precision. Insofar as he identifies the collective unconscious with God and considers living creatures incarnations of God—meant to achieve self-reflection—Jung does, I believe, acknowledge that the *ultimate* Self—now capitalized—is God and, as such, singular and undifferentiated.

However, he also signals his openness to the possibility of there being, *in between* the empirical personality and the ultimate

Self, an *intermediary* self—the meta-daemon—on which we fall back after bodily death; a tru*er* but not ultimate self. For instance, at one point in his autobiography Jung recounts a near-death experience (NDE) he had after a heart attack in 1944. It is abundantly clear in his account that during the NDE, although he had parted with his empirical personality, he retained some form of individual identity (cf. MDR: 320-323), which he refers to as a "primal form" (MDR: 323). Moreover, still in his autobiography, Jung admits to being open to the notion of re-incarnation (cf. MDR: 351), which presupposes the persistence of some form of individual identity after bodily death.

We cannot resolve this issue, but neither is it truly necessary to do so. Even if there are whole hierarchies of intermediary selves between us and God, they, too, will be illusory, for the same reason that Jung tells us the empirical personality is illusory (cf. MDR: 356). What truly matters in Jung's message is the understanding that we are ultimately grounded in something infinite and eternal, and that our lives as finite beings, illusory as they may be, serve a divine purpose.

Chapter 7

Finale

All that doth pass away
Is but a symbol;
The insufficient here
Grows to existence;
The indescribable
Here is it done;
Johann Wolfgang von Goethe, in *Faust* (1832)

Jung's work is a *tour de force* of the psyche, which—remarkably—leads to direct insights into the nature of life and the universe at large. Three key ideas underlie his implicit metaphysical system: first, that of the collective unconscious as a transpersonal experiential field, which generates all autonomous imagery we experience as both the perceived physical world and the worlds of dreams and visions; second, that of consciousness as an internally connected web of psychic contents that turns in upon itself so as to enable self-reflection; and third, that of daemons, autonomous psychic complexes that, although internally connected and conscious, are dissociated from their psychic surroundings.

These three key ideas explain much of the psychiatric phenomenology and psychopathology that Jung had to deal with in his professional practice. The notion of the collective unconscious made sense of the commonality of symbolic themes underlying his patients' dreams and psychotic visions. It also made sense of the uncanny conjunctions—synchronicities—between the contents of his patients' inner lives and the behavior of the physical world surrounding them. The notion of consciousness as a particular experiential *configuration* featuring high internal connectivity and self-reflection explained why much of his patients' psychic lives went unreported: while still experiential, this part of their inner lives wasn't self-reflective or introspectively accessible by the ego. Finally, the notion of intruding daemons made sense not only of certain religious experiences, but also of the neurotic patterns of thinking, feeling and behaving—comparable to what once was called 'possession'—that his patients felt powerless to resist.

Remarkably, these same three ideas also have significant—if latent—explanatory power for making sense *of the universe at large*. Indeed, the collective unconscious—whose innate templates of behavior, or archetypes, organize both the individual psyche and the physical world—explains the nature of the physical world: both our material bodies and the inanimate universe as a whole are the *outer appearance of experiential inner life*. This isn't at all surprising when it comes to our body, for the patterns of our metabolism—e.g. brain activity—are clearly what our experiential inner life, both conscious and unconscious, looks like from the outside. But Jung's metaphysics allows us to elegantly extend this very same notion to *all* matter in the universe, not only that in our bodies, thereby eliminating arbitrary metaphysical discontinuities: the inanimate universe, too, is what the *experiential* dynamisms in the collective unconscious look like from our dissociated, daemonic perspective.

Jung's definition of consciousness as a particular configuration of experience—one entailing an internally-connected web of cognitive associations and self-reflection—allows us to explain the *inanimate* matter in the universe as the outer appearance of experiential but *unconscious* inner life. It also allows us to make sense of the regularity and predictability of nature's behavior: unconscious experiences aren't deliberate or premeditated; they are rather instinctual and, as such, regular and predictable. That's why, unlike our own conscious mentation, the laws of nature are so well ordered and self-consistent.

Finally, Jung's notion of daemons validates many aspects of the world's religious metaphysics. Although you and I are particularly sophisticated daemons with visible bodies, Jung's main motivation for postulating the concept was empirical indications that autonomous complexes, *without a corresponding bodily appearance,* exist in the psychic sphere. In other words, he hypothesized the existence of *discarnate* daemons, which can only be reported through introspection, not perception.

In the context of Figure 4, such discarnate daemons inhabit only the segment of the collective unconscious labeled *mundus archetypus,* not the one labeled *physis.* Although this may look like an inelegant asymmetry in Jung's system, we must not forget that the partition of the collective unconscious into *physis* and *mundus archetypus* is something *we* impose on it, based on *our* perceptual possibilities and limitations; the division doesn't necessarily exist out there, in and of itself.

Indeed, there is no reason to believe that the human perceptual apparatus would have evolved to pick out *every* salient dynamism in the collective unconscious. It is entirely plausible—even expectable—that many of these dynamisms don't have a sufficiently relevant impact on our ability to survive, and so evolution will have ignored them. Whatever our perceptual apparatus *did* evolve to register, we label *physis* or physicality; but that doesn't mean that what it *doesn't* register doesn't exist out there. Our inability to pick out discarnate daemons with our five senses says nothing about the daemons' metaphysical status, but only about our five senses. For all we know, those invisible entities are as real and concrete as a person.

The angels, demons and deities of the world's religious traditions can be interpreted, according to Jung's metaphysics, as discarnate daemons. And indeed—as religions throughout history have insisted upon—they can affect our inner lives both positively and negatively, often dramatically, even though their impact on our bodily survivability is likely very limited. Also as religious traditions insist, they are autonomous agencies with a will, agenda and mental life of their own.

Still as illustrated in Figure 4, we both surround and are surrounded by the collective unconscious. However, as discussed above, the distinction between *physis* and *mundus archetypus* is something *we* impose on nature, not necessarily how nature is structured in and of itself; out there, there is only the collective unconscious *as a whole*. So the division illustrated in Figure 4 ultimately isn't a fair depiction of how things are in themselves. How can we now reconcile this conclusion with the whole train of thought, discussed in previous chapters, that has led to the figure?

The truth is that Figure 4 acquiesces to a metaphysically biased way of seeing things; one that, unfortunately, the spirit of our times forces me to comply with if I am to be understood. In reality, whereas the dynamisms of the collective unconscious we pick out through our five senses—i.e. the *physis*—clearly surround us, the ones we pick out in the form of dreams, visions and drives—i.e. the *mundus archetypus*—only seem to be surrounded by us *insofar as we assume them to exist within our head*. This assumption, however, is merely an artifact of a particular metaphysics—materialism—which Jung rejects and denounces. He clarifies the issue by explaining that the psyche itself has no spatial extension and, therefore, cannot be said to be encompassed by our head:[15]

> While everything else that exists takes up a certain amount of room, the soul [i.e. the psyche] cannot be located in space. ... What bulk can we ascribe to thoughts? Are they small, large, long, thin, heavy, fluid, straight, circular, or what? ... [So] here we are with our immediate experiences of ... something that has taken root in the midst of our measurable, ponderable, three-dimensional reality, that differs bafflingly

from this in every respect and in all its parts, and yet reflects it. (MMSS: 188)

Insofar as our heads are objects in space, we cannot say that the psyche is in our heads; for that which is not in space to begin with cannot be encompassed by spatial boundaries, can it? As such, if we are to do justice to Jung's system and assess it according to its own logic, we must acknowledge that many dreams, visions and compulsions, too, are *external* to us—i.e. they originate outside ego-consciousness—and assail us from without. Our empirical self is thus *always surrounded by the collective unconscious*, as an island in the ocean. Although our personal psyches are rooted in it, the collective unconscious is always out there; it is the experiential environment we inhabit as individual creatures.

Regarding its place in the Western philosophical tradition, Jung's views are broadly consistent with German Idealism. His focus on self-reflection as the meaning of life echoes Georg Hegel's attribution of a central role to self-awareness in universal evolution, as discussed in his (Hegel's) book, *The Phenomenology of Mind* (1807).[16] Concerning its more specific structure and details, Jung's system is well aligned with those of Schopenhauer and yours truly. Readers who notice that Jung's metaphysics—as elucidated in this volume—is incomplete and seemingly inconsistent with certain empirical facts, would do well to peruse both Schopenhauer's work (Schopenhauer & Payne 1969)—or my short summary and elucidation thereof (Kastrup 2020)—and my own (Kastrup 2014, 2016a, 2019). Many answers can be found in these other volumes, resolving the remaining weaknesses and apparent inconsistencies of Jung's system, and generally complementing it.

As a matter of fact, the idealist thought-line linking the works of Schopenhauer (19th century), Jung (20th century) and myself (21st century) reflects a consistent development in the Western philosophical tradition, whose origins are to be found yet farther back in time, crosslinking with Eastern schools such as Advaita Vedanta. Each work in this long idealist tradition reinforces, clarifies and elaborates upon ideas already expressed in other works, together constituting a solid, reliable, robust philosophical platform. The tradition makes clear that metaphysical idealism isn't merely a fashionable, idiosyncratic or ephemeral point of view, but one that the human mind has discerned again and again throughout history, with uncanny consistency, despite the vulgarity and superficiality of the spirit of the time.

Jung's is, of course, the most psychologically sophisticated body of work in the idealist tradition. Its key implication is that *the physical world at large is invested with meaning,* in a semantic sense, just as our dreams presumably are. Allow me to elaborate on this again, for it is an extremely important point.

When we wake up from an intense archetypal dream, such as the muddy monster dream discussed in Chapter 3, we never assume that the dream was exactly what it seemed to be. In other words, we don't wake up thinking that there *literally* was a muddy monster coming from the ocean and destroying everything on its path. We know instead that the dream was a symbolic expression of the psyche. Therefore, we ask ourselves: What did it mean? Why did I dream what I dreamed? What does the dream say about me, the dreamer? That's why many dreamers and psychologists are interested in dream interpretation, the art and science of unveiling the *meaning* of dreams, deciphering their underlying message.

According to Jung's metaphysics, the physical world outside, just like intense nightly dreams, is also a psychic expression organized according to archetypal patterns. We inhabit an experiential universe embodying archetypal semantics. As such, waking life is in many ways akin to a dream *and thus symbolic, non-literal, amenable to interpretation.* Like our nightly dreams, the physical world isn't *just* what it seems to be; instead, it is also an expression of underlying mental dynamisms, therefore carrying a message. Life in the world can be interpreted just as our nightly dreams can. Upon lying in bed at night, after a long day, we may ask ourselves the same question we ask upon waking up from a dream: What did this day mean? *What is the dream we call physical reality saying about its dreamer?* The attempt to answer this question by leveraging our unique ability to *reflect* is our service to God. The universe is God's dream and we are here to interpret it.

At a time when culture and society are dominated by the simplistic, myopic worldview of metaphysical materialism — with its accompanying existential angst — Jung's work offers us a renewed horizon of meaning and purpose: life is sacrificial in the noblest sense imaginable, in that we live and die to render an indispensable service to God. What a great honor and opportunity it is to live.

Jung's legacy is a treasure with the potential to enrich our lives in unsuspected ways, provided that it is discovered and properly understood. Co-opted as it has been by the mainstream — a necessary evil — it must be perused carefully if its true message and implications are to be discerned. The little volume you've now almost finished reading has been my attempt to facilitate such discovery. In this spirit, I leave you with Jung's words:

Nobody can know what the ultimate things are. We must, therefore, take them as we experience them. And if such experience helps to make your life healthier, more beautiful, more complete and more satisfactory to yourself and to those you love, you may safely say: "This was the grace of God." (PR: 114)

Afterword by James Hollis

The modernist revolution, and central to the post-modernist *Weltanschauung* as well, relocates the center of the personality from the narrow sphere of consciousness to a vast iridescent sea of being in which the ego is such a small, tenuous wafer. Carl Jung was one of the pioneers of this project, which attempts to talk about that which cannot be talked about, understand that which cannot be understood. He dared to address the contents of the unconscious, about which, by definition, we can say so little.

Speaking as a Jungian analyst, I have been engaged with Jung's 'metaphysics' for several decades as I, along with so many colleagues, have sought to understand the mazy motions of the unconscious as they spill into the world all around us. If Jung considered life as a kind of interpretable dream, then perhaps working with dreams might allow insights into the nature of our lives, and how we conduct them. As an analyst, I cannot see or hear the unconscious until it manifests in some tangible form—somatic complaint, dream image, behavioral pattern, *et al.* Then I have a chance of working backwards into the realm of the unknown to sense the wounding, the response, the compensatory and healing gestures which psyche has arranged. It is abundantly clear to me, and any who track the peregrinations of psyche, that the psyche is never silent, never. It is always speaking, but it speaks the language of dream, symptom, intuition, insights, and repeatedly provides apertures into the larger mysteries in which we swim.

What I appreciate most about Bernardo Kastrup's approach is his recognition that the tools of philosophy can help us approach the depth, the gift of analytic psychology and appreciate its contributions. The encounter with the psyche is of course phenomenological, experiential; but the artifacts which arise from that experience, the epiphenomenal sequelae, may become available to consciousness, and thus to analytic approach. In the midst of his midlife travails, Jung asked himself how he could dialogue with the energies so insurgent within him, and concluded that he had to attend the secondary phenomena, the images which arose from those telluric sources. Attending the images allowed him to hold the position of consciousness, rather than be swept aside by the power of the unconscious. Attending the images, respectfully attending, allowed that energy its autonomy while offering the gifts of insight and potential re-appropriation of energy.

If metaphysics is an effort to move beyond the sentient data available to consciousness and speculate on its essence, then one may also ask if such insight intimates the nature of all forms beneath, or behind, the plethora of sensory experience. If, as the ancients speculated in the smaragdine tablet of Hermes Trismegistus, things above are copies of things below, then it may also be argued that things below are simulacra of things above. While all of this positions Jung in the long stream of idealism, beginning with Plato, Plotinus, Berkeley, and others, it suggests also that his insight is radically new because it brings to startled awareness a post-Kantian perspective that all that we experience is psychological, that is to say, that it is experienced intra-psychically however much it may be autonomously other. Said succinctly, Kant made phenomenology and depth psychology necessary.

Similarly, Jung anticipated the discoveries of quantum mechanics in his articulation of synchronicity, the intimation of a formative confluence of outer and inner which transcends the Newtonian world of cause and effect. Acausal causality is an insight at least as old as the *I Ching*, and as new as modern physics, but Jung's bold leap is to affirm that the archetype of meaning is just as much a player in the formation of natural events as is the old causality. While such assertions offend the education most of us received mid-twentieth century, we need to re-position ourselves into a world far more mysterious than we have ever thought. As the world of cosmology, physics, and depth psychology become more and more mysterious, so we are brought back to the arena in which all these events occur for us, are processed for us—the human psyche. This is not 'psychologizing,' not reducing all things to the psychological. It means that we are obliged to begin to see the world swathed in mystery again. It demands that we reposition the oft-inflated ego to its proper position of humility.

We would all understand Jung, and depth psychology, much better if we could get out of the ego's ploy, understandable as it might be, of converting energies to objects, process to reified concepts, and verbs to nouns. While it is bad grammar to speak of the Self *selving*, or the archetype *archetyping*, it is far more accurate in understanding Jung's intuitive grasp that the nature of those energies coursing through us are formative, shaping, and in service to rendering the world ordered in meaningful rather than simply chaotic ways.

As an analyst, I work hour by hour trying to decipher the mysteries of dreams, behavioral patterns, somatic images, symptoms, and so on. What I can say, after all these years, is that they all seem in service to some sort of energy system which is transpersonal, and obviously transcendent to ego management. Whether one labels that source *God* or the *Self* or the *Soul* matters little to us, for either way it summons us to observe, pay attention, respect, and learn what is being taught us. It asks us to consider what is seeking to unfold within and through us, quite outside ego volition and conscious direction.

It is not so radical to imagine then that what we discern gives us insight into the formative energies that course through all of nature, all of history. Those are the same energies, and the same epiphenomenal manifestations, which have drawn the attention of theologians, metaphysicians, physicists, and all of us to attendance throughout history. Kastrup's decoding of Jung's profound insights adds another layer to our understanding. Rather than see, post-Kant, metaphysics as wistful speculation, one sees that the *meta-physis* engagement has moved within, where it always was.

James Hollis, Ph.D.
Washington, D.C.

Appendix: The Fall

Jung makes occasional references to the biblical Fall of Man—the eating of the forbidden fruit from the tree of knowledge in paradise—as a symbol of the development of consciousness. This seemingly innocent mythical reference evokes seminal events from our prehistory; mysterious events that continue to reverberate today, for they are the primal source not only of our unique cognitive capacities amongst animals, but also of our suffering. I shall elaborate on all this in what follows.

An early and relatively extensive passage of Jung's wherein he makes reference to the biblical Fall can be found in an essay titled "The Stages of Life" (MMSS: 97-116). Having defined 'problems' as "things that are difficult, questionable or ambiguous" (MMSS: 97), he continues:

> It is the growth of consciousness which we must thank for the existence of problems; ... As long as we are still submerged in nature we are unconscious, and we live in the security of instinct that knows no problems. (MMSS: 98)

Instinctual animals face no dilemmas or difficult choices; instead, instinct always provides them with *one*, clear path forward. They don't second-guess themselves, regret past choices or feel anxiety about future predicaments. By operating purely instinctually they are one with nature and feel no inner tension. Only we, conscious human beings, do all those things, for "we have turned away from the certain guidance of instinct and are handed over to fear" (MMSS: 98). Consciousness is what makes us *suffer*. The development of consciousness

> is the *sacrifice* of the merely natural man—of the unconscious, ingenuous being ... *The biblical fall of man presents the dawn of*

consciousness as a curse. (MMSS: 98-99, emphasis added)

This is an extraordinary passage. Jung is saying that attaining consciousness—the Fall of Man—is a curse, which he later characterizes as our sacrifice to God, to help God develop self-reflection. The unspoken implication is that, insofar as the devil tricked Adam and Eve into taking a bite from the forbidden fruit, it was the devil who sacrificed humans, so as to render a service to his father. And since hatching such a plan must have required *foresight*—a capability unique to consciousness—presumably the devil had already sacrificed *himself*. Indeed, Jung gives plenty of hints in *Answer to Job* that, in his view, this was the case:

> Satan who, with good reason, later on received the name of "Lucifer" [i.e. bringer of light[17]], knew how to make more frequent and better use of omniscience than did his father. (AJ: 51)

Satan, the chief tormentor, as the original *tormented*; demons as the tough-love instigators of self-awareness (which is, in fact, how they are often portrayed in popular culture, if one pays attention): the symbolism of the Genesis story is extremely rich, and Jung knew it.

At the time he wrote his essay on the stages of life, however, Jung's ideas about the nature of consciousness were still incomplete and evolving. Taking a cue from the name of the tree that produced the forbidden fruit—the 'tree of knowledge'— he links consciousness to contextual knowledge, i.e. webs of cognitively associated contents, apparently overlooking self-reflection:

> There are no problems without consciousness. We must therefore put the question in another way: In what way does consciousness arise? ... when a child recognizes someone or

something—when he "knows" a person or a thing—then we feel that the child has consciousness. That, no doubt, is also why in Paradise it was the tree of knowledge which bore such fateful fruit. (MMSS: 100)

By insisting on knowledge, Jung may be implicitly—even unconsciously—assuming Schopenhauer's definition thereof, with which we know he was acquainted. Indeed, for Schopenhauer knowledge *already entails a degree of self-reflection,* a separation between subject and object (cf. Kastrup 2020). It is by *reflecting*— re-representing—an initial experience on a higher level of cognition that we separate ourselves, as know*ing* subjects, from our know*n* experiences. This is why we say that we *have* pain, or *see* an object, or *feel* love. In other words, we are that on which the pain, the object and the love are meta-cognitively *reflected.* Without this reflection, we would effectively *be* the pain, the object and the love; there would be no cognizable difference between the experience and the experienc*er.*

In fact, the Bible itself is already very clear about the nature of the knowledge provided by the fateful tree. There we are told that Adam and Eve, before they ate from the forbidden fruit, "were both naked, and were not ashamed" (Genesis, 2:25).[18] So although Adam and Eve were not blind to their own nakedness— presumably they *experienced* it all the time—their cognition of this nakedness somehow did not trigger the shame it would trigger in most of us, conscious human beings. Adam and Eve did have the experience of being naked, but not quite in the same way you and I would have it.

Then the devil, disguised as a serpent, tells Eve: "when you eat of [the fruit of the tree of knowledge] your eyes will be opened" (Genesis, 3:5). Yet Eve's eyes were presumably already open; she wasn't blind. The devil obviously meant something *more* than just perceptual experience here.

I suggest that the fruit of the tree of knowledge conferred a *self-reflective* mode of cognition on Adam and Eve. Eating from the fruit developed in them not the ability to experience things — which they already had — but to know *that* they experienced things. It enabled them to recognize themselves as *those who experience* — i.e. as subjects — as opposed to the experiences themselves. Prior to acquiring this ability, they could already experience nakedness, but they didn't know *that* they experienced nakedness. Therefore, they felt no shame. From the Bible:

> So when the woman saw that the tree was good for food, and that it was a delight to the eyes, and that the tree was to be desired to make one wise, she took of its fruit and ate; and she also gave some to her husband, who was with her, and he ate. Then the eyes of both were opened, *and they knew* that *they were naked*. (Genesis, 3:6-7, emphasis added)

Precisely! Only then did they know *that* they were naked, in a self-reflective manner, even though they had already, all along, been experiencing their nakedness. *The Fall was the fall into self-reflection.*

Psychologists know that self-reflection is associated with our uniquely human ability to think *symbolically* — i.e. to process the contents of consciousness through the mediation of internal pointers, such as words, so as to tell ourselves in language what we are experiencing and thereby deliberately plan our actions. Alex Gillespie gives an example:

> In order to obtain dinner one must first name ... one's hunger ... This naming, *which is a moment of self-reflection,* is the first step in beginning to construct, semiotically, a path of action that will lead to dinner. (Gillespie 2007: 678, emphasis added)

The emergence of symbolic thinking in us humans *is the Fall;* it was precisely what differentiated us from the "unconscious, ingenuous being" we originally were, guided purely by instinct and without problems.

Remarkably, paleoanthropologists today know that the first modern humans, anatomically indistinguishable from us, did *not* originally have the capacity for symbolic thinking we now do. In the words of Ian Tattersall, curator of the Hall of Human Origins of the American Museum of Natural History,

> As far as *Homo sapiens* is concerned it appears that body form was one thing, while the symbolic cognitive system that distinguishes us so greatly from all other creatures was entirely another. The two were not acquired at the same time [!], and the earliest anatomical *Homo sapiens* appear right now to have been cognitively indistinguishable from Neanderthals and other contemporaries. (Tattersall 2012: 185-186)

So when we fell into self-reflection we were already physically what we are today. We didn't fall into humanity; *we fell as humans.* The Fall is an *actual pre-historical event*, even though one shrouded in mystery:

> Our ancestors made an almost unimaginable transition from a non-symbolic, nonlinguistic way of processing and communicating information about the world to the symbolic and linguistic condition we enjoy today. It is a qualitative leap in cognitive state unparalleled in history. Indeed, ... the only reason we have for believing that such a leap *could* ever have been made, is that it *was* made. (Tattersall 2012: 199, original emphasis)

It boggles the mind how unlikely the Fall was, for

> our novel way of dealing with information was *hardly a predictable outcome of any identifiable trend that preceded it.*

And neither was it simply a threshold effect of acquiring a greater and greater brain volume over vast spans of time … it seems overwhelmingly likely that … our cognitive ability was acquired as a *byproduct* of the hugely ramifying genetic *accident* that resulted in the appearance of *Homo sapiens* … the potential it created then lay fallow for a substantial length of time, until its symbolic potential was 'discovered' by its owner. (Tattersall 2012: 208-210, emphasis added)

Well, synchronicity then! No, really, pause for a moment to allow the significance of the statement quoted above to sink in: Tattersall is telling us here that there was *no direct selective pressure* to fix our ability to think symbolically—and, therefore, to self-reflect—in our genome. At first, and then "for a substantial length of time," it didn't help us survive at all. So we do not actually understand how or why we've come to have it in the first place. The best we can say is that it was all an accident, which for tens of thousands of years was basically useless.

The bottom-line is, *we currently have no natural explanation for our fall into self-reflection.* As far as we know, it was an 'act of God'…

… Or, of course, of the devil, for the Bible tells us that the devil was behind the whole affair. The chief angel of God, *who fell first,* was set on helping his father develop self-reflective introspection, so he (God) could finally *consult* his omniscience deliberately (cf. AJ: 49). The devil then used us to accomplish his goal. And as a result of falling for such a devilish trap, we were—and are still being—severely punished:

cursed is the ground because of you; in toil you shall eat of it all the days of your life; thorns and thistles it shall bring forth for you; and you shall eat the plants of the field. By the sweat of your face you shall eat bread until you return to the ground, for out of it you were taken; you are dust, and to dust you shall return. (Genesis, 3:17-19)

And then,

> the LORD God sent him [Adam] forth from the garden of Eden, to till the ground from which he was taken. He drove out the man; and at the east of the garden of Eden he placed the cherubim, and a sword flaming and turning to guard the way to the tree of life. (Genesis, 3:23-24)

The exile from paradise marked the end of the unconscious human being, living from instinct with no problems, and the beginning of psychological suffering. The Fall represents the inception of our lives of sacrifice to God.

How can the acquisition of self-reflection lead to so much suffering? The answer is not difficult to see. It is self-reflection that allows us to recognize our own limited condition as mortal creatures, which in turn enables us to create narratives about self and world. We compulsively produce stories about what the past should have been, leading to regret, bitterness, disappointment, anger and a general inability to let go. We also compulsively produce stories about what the future might yet be, leading to anxiety and fear. Before the Fall, we lived solely in the present moment, in unity with nature, like the other animals in paradise.

The exile from paradise led to suffering because, from that point on, we began to compare reality to imagined alternative scenarios, 'alternative realities' of our own creation. But who has the power to create realities? God, of course. So "when you eat of [the fruit of the tree of knowledge] your eyes will be opened, *and you will be like God*" (Genesis, 3:5, emphasis added).

Self-reflection allows us to leave the immediacy of the present moment by imagining past and future scenarios, which we then torture ourselves with. We fell when the forbidden fruit gave us the ability to create internal narratives about what should have been and what might yet be. We've become addicted to using these self-manufactured alternatives to struggle against what is. And such futile struggle is what generates all psychological suffering.

Yet, it is the same struggle that sharpens our consciousness and enables us to render a service to God. Each problem "forces us to *greater consciousness*" (MMSS: 99, emphasis added); each helps us help God. After all, the tree is supposedly "the tree of the knowledge of good and evil" (Genesis, 2:9), not only of evil. Through this knowledge of good—the re-representation of creation on the mirror of self-reflection—we help God become aware of itself.

Ours are indeed sacrificial lives, therein residing their profound meaning.

Notes

1 A *daemon* is not to be conflated with a 'demon,' in the modern meaning of the word. Daemons do not *necessarily* have—though they *may* have—any bias toward either good or evil. They are prompting or instigating agencies, usually overwhelming, but often morally neutral.

2 Jung's implicit reference point here is our ego, the segment of the psyche which we identify with. As such, the objective psyche is objective *relative to the ego*. Relative to itself, however—as I shall discuss shortly—the objective psyche may very well entail a form of subjectivity.

3 We shall later see that this particular analogy is central to Jung's metaphysics.

4 For this reason, I shall henceforth use the terms 'meta-consciousness' and 'self-reflection' interchangeably, in the sense of phenomenally conscious meta-cognition.

5 Both the Jewish and Islamic traditions incorporate this noble principle. For a discussion, see the online essay "The Origins of the Precept 'Whoever Saves a Life Saves the World' and what they tell us about particularism and universalism in Jewish tradition," published in *Mosaic magazine* on 31 October 2016 and available at https://mosaicmagazine. com/observation/history-ideas/2016/10/the-origins-of-the-precept-whoever-saves-a-life-saves-the-world/ (accessed 22 September 2019).

6 The 'butterfly effect' happens when a complex, non-linear system—such as, for instance, the weather—is so sensitive to its initial conditions that tiny perturbations in these conditions can lead to very large differences in outcome. The classical hypothetical example is that of the flapping of a butterfly's wings leading to a tornado weeks later.

7 As we shall soon see, for Jung and Pauli these events weren't

accidents at all. They obeyed, instead, another organizing principle different from causality. But because we currently do not recognize such principle, we are forced to attribute all existence, including ourselves, to mere accidents.

8   In an earlier work, Jung talks of "the final transformation of the yogin's consciousness into the *divine all-consciousness*" (PR: 82, emphasis added) alluded to in Eastern philosophy and spiritual practices, which touches on the same idea of a unitary universal consciousness underlying all existence. Clearly, Jung had already been well acquainted with this notion for some time before he wrote about synchronicity.

9   Indeed, materialism makes statements about what nature *is* in and of itself—namely, matter outside and independent of experience—not about how nature *behaves*. Science, in turn, occupies itself only with the latter question.

10 The central recognition behind the 'hard problem' is that there is nothing about matter, energy or arrangements thereof *in terms of which* one could deduce—at least in principle—what it *feels* like to see red, taste strawberries, have a bellyache or fall in love. More specifically, nothing we can observe or measure about the arrangement of atoms constituting the brain reveals what it feels like to see red or to fall in love. The domain of experience, with its *qualities*, is incommensurable with the domain of physicality, defined by measurable *quantities*. As such, the psyche cannot be reduced to physicality.

11 Eliminative materialism is the view that some or even *all* experiences posited by common-sense do not actually exist. In its strongest form, eliminative materialism claims, absurdly, that "Consciousness doesn't happen. It's a mistaken construct" (Graziano 2016).

12 In a crossed-out sentence of a letter to Fr. White, Jung contrasts what he calls *"Ideen Realismus"* (the independent, autonomous reality of ideas) with *"Ideen Materialismus"* (the

notion that ideas are real only insofar as they are concretized in matter), clearly identifying himself with the former (JWL: 158). *"Ideen Realismus"* would today be called 'objective idealism' by philosophers (cf. Chalmers 2018).

13   Jung makes the same point in an earlier work (PR: 12).

14   A rare, subtle but highly suggestive passage wherein Jung hints at the relationship between God and the archetypal god-image in the human psyche is this: "when I say as a psychologist that God is an archetype, I mean by that the 'type' in the psyche. The word 'type' is, as we know, derived from τύπος, 'blow' or 'imprint'; *thus an archetype presupposes an imprinter"* (PA: 14, emphasis added). The suggestion, of course, is that God is what imprints the archetypal god-image in the human psyche, even though Jung rushes to say that psychology, as a science, cannot outright make such an assertion.

15   There are other passages wherein Jung suggests that psychic dynamisms are not comprised in spacetime (cf. e.g. PA: 105 & 182).

16   The original title of Hegel's book is *Phänomenologie des Geistes*, which is most often translated as *The Phenomenology of Spirit*. However, I believe the correct translation of the German word *Geistes* in the context of Hegel's argument is 'Mind.'

17   According to Jung, light is a symbol of consciousness (cf. e.g. PA: 186). So the bringer of light is a bringer of consciousness.

18   All bible quotes in this appendix are taken from the Vatican's website.

Bibliography

Block, N. (1995). On a confusion about a function of consciousness. *Behavioral and Brain Sciences*, 18: 227-287.

Campbell, J. (2008). *The Hero with a Thousand Faces.* Novato, CA: New World Library.

Cardeña, E. (2018). The experimental evidence for parapsychological phenomena: A review. *American Psychologist*, 73 (5): 663-677.

Chalmers, D. (1995). Facing up to the problem of consciousness. *Journal of Consciousness Studies*, 2 (3): 200-219.

Chalmers, D. (2018). Idealism and the mind-body problem. In: Seager, W. (ed.). *The Routledge Handbook of Panpsychism.* London, UK: Routledge.

Clay, C. (2016). *Labyrinths: Emma Jung, Her Marriage to Carl, and the Early Years of Psychoanalysis.* New York, NY: HarperCollins.

Elk, M. van, Friston, K. and Bekkering, H. (2016). The Experience of Coincidence: An Integrated Psychological and Neurocognitive Perspective. In: Landsman, K. and Wolde, E. van (eds.). *The Challenge of Chance: The Frontiers Collection.* Cham, Switzerland: Springer.

Franz, M.-L. von (1974). *Number and Time: Reflections leading toward a unification of depth psychology and physics.* Evanston: Northwestern University Press.

Gillespie, A. (2007). The social basis of self-reflection. In: Valsiner, J. and Rosa, A. (eds.). *The Cambridge Handbook of Sociocultural Psychology.* New York, NY: Cambridge University Press, pp. 678-691.

Graziano, M. (2016). Consciousness is not mysterious. *The Atlantic*, 12 January. [Online]. Available from: http://www.theatlantic.com/science/archive/2016/01/consciousness-color-brain/423522/ [Accessed 10 August 2019].

Gu, M. *et al.* (2009). More really is different. *Physica D: Nonlinear*

Phenomena, 238 (9-10): 835-839.

Joos, E. (2006). The Emergence of Classicality from Quantum Theory. In: Clayton, P. and Davies, P. (editors). *The Re-Emergence of Emergence: The Emergentist Hypothesis from Science to Religion*. Oxford, UK: Oxford University Press.

Jung, C. G. (author), Adler, G. and Jaffé, A. (editors) (1975). *C. G. Jung Letters*. Princeton, NJ: Princeton University Press.

Jung, C. G. (1977). *Psychology and Religion*. New Haven, CT: Yale University Press.

Jung, C. G. (1978). *Flying Saucers: A Modern Myth of Things Seen in the Skies*. Princeton, NJ: Princeton University Press.

Jung, C. G. (1979). *Aion, 2ⁿᵈ Ed*. Princeton, NJ: Princeton University Press.

Jung, C. G. (1980). *Psychology and Alchemy, 2ⁿᵈ Edition*. London, UK: Routledge.

Jung, C. G. (1985). *Synchronicity: An Acausal Connecting Principle*. London, UK: Routledge.

Jung, C. G. (1991). *The Archetypes and the Collective Unconscious*. London, UK: Routledge.

Jung, C. G. (author) and Jaffé, A. (editor) (1995). *Memories, Dreams, Reflections*. London, UK: Fontana Press.

Jung, C. G., Pauli, W. (authors) and Meier, C. A. (editor) (2001). *Atom and Archetype: The Pauli/Jung Letters 1932-1958*. London, UK: Routledge.

Jung, C. G. (2001). *Dreams*. London, UK: Routledge.

Jung, C. G. (2001). *Modern Man in Search of a Soul*. London, UK: Routledge.

Jung, C. G. (2001). *On the Nature of the Psyche*. London, UK: Routledge.

Jung, C. G. (2002). *Answer to Job*. London, UK: Routledge.

Jung, C. G. (2002). *The Undiscovered Self*. London, UK: Routledge.

Jung, C. G., White, V. (authors), Lammers, A. C. and Cunningham, A. (editors) (2007). *The Jung-White Letters*. London, UK: Routledge.

Jung, C. G. (author) and Shamdasani, S. (editor) (2009). *The Red Book: Liber Novus*. London, UK: W. W. Norton & Company.

Kastrup, B. (2011). *Rationalist Spirituality: An exploration of the meaning of life and existence informed by logic and science*. Winchester, UK: Iff Books.

Kastrup, B. (2014). *Why Materialism Is Baloney: How true skeptics know there is no death and fathom answers to life, the universe, and everything*. Winchester, UK: Iff Books.

Kastrup, B. (2016a). *More Than Allegory: On religious myth, truth and belief*. Winchester, UK: Iff Books.

Kastrup, B. (2016b). The physicalist worldview as neurotic ego-defense mechanism. *SAGE Open*, doi: 10.1177/2158244016674515.

Kastrup, B. (2018). Conflating abstraction with empirical observation: The false mind-matter dichotomy. *Constructivist Foundations*, 13 (3): 341-361.

Kastrup, B. (2019). *The Idea of the World: A multi-disciplinary argument for the mental nature of reality*. Winchester, UK: Iff Books.

Kastrup, B. (2020). *Decoding Schopenhauer's Metaphysics: The key to understanding how it solves the hard problem of consciousness and the paradoxes of quantum mechanics*. Winchester, UK: Iff Books.

Kingsley, P. (2018). *Catafalque: Carl Jung and the end of humanity*. London, UK: Catafalque Press.

Lloyd, S. (2006). *Programming the Universe: A quantum computer scientist takes on the cosmos*. New York, NY: Alfred A. Knopf.

Russell, B. (2009). *Human Knowledge: Its Scope and Limits*. London, UK: Routledge Classics.

Schlumpf, Y. *et al.* (2014). Dissociative part-dependent resting-state activity in Dissociative Identity Disorder: A controlled fMRI perfusion study. *PloS ONE*, 9, doi:10.1371/journal.pone.0098795.

Schooler, J. (2002). Re-representing consciousness: Dissociations between experience and meta-consciousness. *Trends in Cognitive Sciences*, 6 (8): 339-344.

Schopenhauer, A. (author) and Payne, E. F. J. (translator) (1969). *The World as Will and Representation*. New York, NY: Dover Publications, Inc.

Stevens, A. (2001). *Jung: A Very Short Introduction*. Oxford, UK: Oxford University Press.

Strasburger, H. and Waldvogel, B. (2015). Sight and blindness in the same person: Gating in the visual system. *PsyCh Journal*, 4 (4): 178-185.

Stubenberg, L. (2018). Neutral Monism. In: Zalta, E. (ed.). The Stanford Encyclopedia of Philosophy (Fall 2018 Edition). [Online]. Available from: https://plato.stanford.edu/archives/fall2018/entries/neutral-monism [Accessed 3 August 2019].

Tattersall, I. (2012). *Masters of the Planet: The search for our human origins*. New York, NY: Palgrave MacMillan.

Taylor, C. (2007). *A Secular Age*. Cambridge, MA: Harvard University Press.

Tsuchiya, N. *et al.* (2015). No-report paradigms: Extracting the true neural correlates of consciousness. *Trends in Cognitive Sciences*, 19 (12): 757-770.

Vandenbroucke, A. *et al.* (2014). Seeing without knowing: Neural signatures of perceptual inference in the absence of report. *Journal of Cognitive Neuroscience*, 26 (5): 955-969.

Wigner, E. (1960). The Unreasonable Effectiveness of Mathematics in the Natural Sciences. *Communications on Pure and Applied Mathematics*, 13 (1): 1-14.

Windt, J. M. and Metzinger, T. (2007). The philosophy of dreaming and self-consciousness: what happens to the experiential subject during the dream state? In: Barrett, D. and McNamara, P. (eds.). *The New Science of Dreaming*. Westport, CT: Praeger, pp. 193-247.

ACADEMIC AND SPECIALIST

Iff Books publishes non-fiction. It aims to work with authors and titles that augment our understanding of the human condition, society and civilisation, and the world or universe in which we live.
If you have enjoyed this book, why not tell other readers by posting a review on your preferred book site.
Recent bestsellers from Iff Books are:

Why Materialism Is Baloney
How true skeptics know there is no death and fathom answers to life, the universe, and everything
Bernardo Kastrup
A hard-nosed, logical, and skeptic non-materialist metaphysics, according to which the body is in mind, not mind in the body.
Paperback: 978-1-78279-362-5 ebook: 978-1-78279-361-8

The Fall
Steve Taylor
The Fall discusses human achievement versus the issues of war, patriarchy and social inequality.
Paperback: 978-1-78535-804-3 ebook: 978-1-78535-805-0

Brief Peeks Beyond
Critical essays on metaphysics, neuroscience, free will, skepticism and culture
Bernardo Kastrup
An incisive, original, compelling alternative to current mainstream cultural views and assumptions.
Paperback: 978-1-78535-018-4 ebook: 978-1-78535-019-1

Framespotting
Changing how you look at things changes how
you see them
Laurence & Alison Matthews
A punchy, upbeat guide to framespotting. Spot deceptions and
hidden assumptions; swap growth for growing up. See and be free.
Paperback: 978-1-78279-689-3 ebook: 978-1-78279-822-4

Is There an Afterlife?
David Fontana
Is there an Afterlife? If so what is it like? How do Western ideas
of the afterlife compare with Eastern? David Fontana presents
the historical and contemporary evidence for survival of physical
death.
Paperback: 978-1-90381-690-5

Nothing Matters
a book about nothing
Ronald Green
Thinking about Nothing opens the world to everything by
illuminating new angles to old problems and stimulating new
ways of thinking.
Paperback: 978-1-84694-707-0 ebook: 978-1-78099-016-3

Panpsychism
The Philosophy of the Sensuous Cosmos
Peter Ells
Are free will and mind chimeras? This book, anti-materialistic
but respecting science, answers: No! Mind is foundational to all
existence.
Paperback: 978-1-84694-505-2 ebook: 978-1-78099-018-7

Punk Science
Inside the Mind of God
Manjir Samanta-Laughton
Many have experienced unexplainable phenomena; God, psychic
abilities, extraordinary healing and angelic encounters. Can
cutting-edge science actually explain phenomena
previously thought of as 'paranormal'?
Paperback: 978-1-90504-793-2

The Vagabond Spirit of Poetry
Edward Clarke
Spend time with the wisest poets of the modern age and of the
past, and let Edward Clarke remind you of the importance of
poetry in our industrialized world.
Paperback: 978-1-78279-370-0 ebook: 978-1-78279-369-4

Readers of ebooks can buy or view any of these bestsellers by
clicking on the live link in the title. Most titles are published in
paperback and as an ebook. Paperbacks are available in traditional
bookshops. Both print and ebook formats are available online.
Find more titles and sign up to our readers' newsletter at
http://www.johnhuntpublishing.com/non-fiction
Follow us on Facebook at
https://www.facebook.com/JHPNonFiction
and Twitter at https://twitter.com/JHPNonFiction